WORLD
WAR II

WORLD WAR II

GREAT SPEECHES IN HISTORY

Thomas Streissguth,
Book Editor

Daniel Leone, *President*

Bonnie Szumski, *Publisher*

Scott Barbour, *Managing Editor*

GREENHAVEN
PRESS®

THOMSON
™
GALE

San Diego • Detroit • New York • San Francisco • Cleveland
New Haven, Conn. • Waterville, Maine • London • Munich

LIBRARY OF CONGRESS CATALOGING-IN-PUBLICATION DATA

World War II / Thomas Streissguth, book editor.
   p. cm. — (Greenhaven Press's great speeches in history)
   Includes bibliographical references and index.
   ISBN 0-7377-0879-4 (lib. bdg. : alk. paper) —
   ISBN 0-7377-0878-6 (pbk. : alk. paper)
   1. World War, 1939–1945—Sources. 2. Speeches, addresses, etc. I. Title: World War Two. II. Title: World War 2. III. Streissguth, Thomas, 1958– . IV. Great speeches in history series.
   D741 .W66 2003
   940.53—dc21

2002070623

Contents

and the Finns will fight back with all the skill and
tenacity they are capable of.

Foreword

I have a dream that one day this nation will rise up and live out the true meaning of its creed: "We hold these truths to be self-evident: that all men are created equal."

I have a dream that one day on the red hills of Georgia the sons of former slaves and the sons of former slave owners will be able to sit down together at the table of brotherhood.

I have a dream that one day even the state of Mississippi, a state sweltering with the heat of injustice, sweltering with the heat of oppression, will be transformed into an oasis of freedom and justice.

I have a dream that my four little children will one day live in a nation where they will not be judged by the color of their skin but by the content of their character.

Perhaps no speech in American history resonates as deeply as Martin Luther King Jr.'s "I Have a Dream," delivered in 1963 before a rapt audience of 250,000 on the steps of the Lincoln Memorial in Washington, D.C. Decades later, the speech still enthralls those who read or hear it, and stands as a philosophical guidepost for contemporary discourse on racism.

What distinguishes "I Have a Dream" from the hundreds of other speeches given during the civil rights era are King's eloquence, lyricism, and use of vivid metaphors to convey abstract ideas. Moreover, "I Have a Dream" serves not only as a record of history—a testimony to the racism that permeated American society during the 1960s—but it is also a historical event in its own right. King's speech, aired live on national television, marked the first time that the grave injustice of racism was fully articulated to a mass audience in a way that was both logical and evocative. Julian Bond, a fellow participant in the civil rights movement and student of King's, states that

> King's dramatic 1963 "I Have a Dream" speech before the Lincoln Memorial cemented his place as first among equals in civil rights leadership; from this first televised mass meeting, an American audience saw and heard the unedited oratory of America's finest preacher, and for the first time, a mass white audience heard the undeniable justice of black demands.

Moreover, by helping people to understand the justice of the civil rights movement's demands, King's speech helped to transform the nation. In 1964, a year after the speech was delivered, President Lyndon B. Johnson signed the Civil Rights Act, which outlawed segregation in public facilities and discrimination in employment. In 1965, Congress passed the Voting Rights Act, which forbids restrictions, such as literacy tests, that were commonly used in the South to prevent blacks from voting. King's impact on the country's laws illustrates the power of speech to bring about real change.

Greenhaven Press's Great Speeches in History series offers students an opportunity to read and study some of the greatest speeches ever delivered before an audience. Each volume traces a specific historical era, event, or theme through speeches—both famous and lesser known. An introductory essay sets the stage by presenting background and context. Then a collection of speeches follows, grouped in chapters based on chronology or theme. Each selection is preceded by a brief introduction that offers historical context, biographical information about the speaker, and analysis of the speech. A comprehensive index and an annotated table of contents help readers quickly locate material of interest, and a bibliography serves as a launching point for further research. Finally, an appendix of author biographies provides detailed background on each speaker's life and work. Taken together, the volumes in the Greenhaven Great Speeches in History series offer students vibrant illustrations of history and demonstrate the potency of the spoken word. By reading speeches in their historical context, students will be transported back in time and gain a deeper understanding of the issues that confronted people of the past.

Introduction

On the morning of November 11, 1918, the nations fighting World War I agreed to an armistice. By the terms of the treaty concluded at Versailles, France, the next year, Germany dismantled its military, ceded certain territories to its neighbors, admitted responsibility for beginning the war, and agreed to pay a very heavy sum in reparations. The treaty also called for the formation of the League of Nations, an organization given its form and purpose by the president of the United States, Woodrow Wilson. The dream of Wilson, and the hope of the Allied powers that had just defeated Germany, was that this international league would prevent future world conflict through negotiation, diplomacy, and, if necessary, economic sanctions against aggressor nations.

Through the 1920s, several more treaties were signed as the most powerful nations of the world tried to strike a careful balance of military power. In the meantime, the beaten German nation went through social revolution and economic chaos. By the middle of the 1920s, the country was sliding into an economic abyss. German money lost all value; the humiliating concessions and reparations payments drained the country's treasury; a wave of street riots and aborted revolutions roiled German society while the government ineffectually railed at the Treaty of Versailles and its former World War I opponents.

The depression in Germany was a small and local foretaste of a much greater economic catastrophe, a worldwide depression that took hold during the early 1930s. The Great Depression began with a failure of banks in Europe and the crash of the stock market in the United States. The economic collapse spread to nearly every level of Western society, personal savings accounts were erased and industrial production and trade tumbled, bringing mass unemployment and hunger.

The war and the subsequent depression caused widespread suspicion that all was not right with democracy or with free-market capitalism—two sacrosanct pillars of Western modernism—and that the world might be able to come up with a better alternative. In Russia, the czar and his imperial government had been overthrown and abruptly replaced by Communist revolutionaries who held to the doctrine of socialism: centralized authority over the economy and all means of production. Italy and Germany adopted a different species of totalitarianism known as fascism, a hybrid of nationalism and socialism, that eventually put these two allies and the rest of Europe on another military collision course.

Opening Shots

Benito Mussolini had established the Fascist Party of Italy during the 1920s. His government allowed no elections and no rival parties; his ministers decried the sloppy, uncertain results of multiparty democracy and turned the nation's economy to the production of armaments and its foreign policy to conquest. Much beholden to Mussolini was Adolf Hitler, an Austrian-born World War I veteran who had fought and been injured in the service of Germany. A charismatic rabble-rouser, Hitler promised, if elected as the leader of his adopted country, to bring Germany up and out of the humiliating defeat suffered at Versailles and return the country to its former starring role on the stage of history. The National Socialist German Workers' (Nazi) Party, seized by Hitler during the mid-1920s, attracted hundreds and then thousands of new members as Germany continued its long economic slide.

Hitler attained the first of his goals in January 1933, when his party won a slight majority in Germany's legislative elections. Appointed chancellor, as was legal and customary, by the ailing and aging President Paul von Hindenburg, Hitler quickly welded Germany into a fascist state while rearming that nation in violation of the Versailles treaty. He also promised to return the territories lost to the World War I Allies to German sovereignty.

The militaristic spirit that Hitler brought to Germany echoed a similar phenomenon in eastern Asia, where Japan had begun expanding into the northern Chinese territory of Manchuria in 1931. Japan, like Germany, saw itself as a natural leader and as the master of its corner of the world. According to Japanese leaders, who were held in semidivine reverence by the population, the Japanese nation, so poor in natural resources, had to expand and conquer in order to survive and fulfill its historical role as the master state of Asia. To this end, the Japanese army began a permanent occupation of Manchuria, and Japanese leaders began planning for the occupation of Chinese ports and the conquest of Southeast Asia and the entire western rim of the Pacific Ocean.

Mussolini and Hitler were fascist allies and charismatic leaders. Both promised their homelands glorious victories.

The drive to conquer and rule new territory was essential to totalitarian government in both Italy and Germany. The fascists ruled nearly every facet of their society and their culture; they could not abide political debate, dissenting opinion, or personal freedom. They used all the powers of the police and the courts to carry out this task; in the end, however, the only way to maintain such a harsh grip on a large and industrialized modern nation was to instill within it the ideals of self-sacrifice in the service of the state and of a just military campaign. Hitler and Mussolini both reinforced obedience with a merciless police state, a promise of vengeance for past wrongs, and grandiose claims of national destiny.

Mussolini was the first to strike by attacking the former Italian colony of Ethiopia in 1935. Claiming that his country was the aggrieved party, and that he was only asserting a natural right of the strong to rule the weak, Mussolini ordered a lightning military campaign that quickly subdued the outgunned Ethiopian defenders. Hitler followed Mussolini's example by ordering military conscription in 1935; at the same time, German factories were working at full capacity, turning out tanks and other armored vehicles, airplanes, submarines, artillery, and munitions. This open defiance of the Treaty of Versailles, which limited the German army to one hundred thousand men, was met with protests but no action by the other treaty signatories, who bought a diplomatic truce by announcing that the treaty's limits on military aircraft and submarines were no longer in effect. In March 1936 Hitler tested his opponents again by ordering his army into a "demilitarized" zone established west of the Rhine River, a region bordering France that had been placed off-limits to German forces by the Treaty of Versailles.

The leaders of Germany, Italy, and Japan saw their interests converging, and the unopposed remilitarization of Germany inspired Hitler to strike a pact with Japan in 1936, in which the two nations agreed to resist the spread of communism. A civil war in Spain then allowed Hitler to come to the aid of a fascist ally, General Francisco Franco, while the other governments of western Europe made the decision to stand down from the conflict, as recounted by historian Piers Brendon:

> The governments in London, Paris and Washington . . . were determined not to become embroiled in war on account of Spain . . . The democracies . . . reckoned that the

opposing forces stood for different forms of tyranny . . . Most British Conservatives, although less extreme than the French Right, regarded the civil war as a matter of "Rebel versus Rabble." But both governments, who wanted to protect their large Spanish commercial interests, feared that a Republican [anti-fascist] victory would turn Spain Red. As anxious to contain Communism as to contain war, they embraced neutrality.

The Spanish Civil War resulted in a victory for Franco, and by proxy a victory for his fascist allies in Germany and Italy. In 1937 Italy joined the alliance of Germany and Japan, establishing what came to be known as the Rome-Berlin-Tokyo Axis, or Axis powers. From this point forward the three nations saw their common interest in military and economic cooperation, as well as conquest of weaker neighbors, through diplomacy and then through war, for the sake of land and natural resources.

After the Axis was established, Hitler turned to his southern neighbor, Austria, a nation held off-limits to Germany by the Treaty of Versailles. In the Austrian capital of Vienna,

Hitler had struggled as a young painter and as a wounded war veteran; it was in this city that a personal defeat and a national humiliation had stoked his thirst for vengeance and conquest. He saw the smaller country's destiny tied irrevocably to that of Germany, and to this end he had supported a Nazi underground that had propagandized on his behalf and had assassinated its leading opponent, Chancellor Engelbert Dollfuss, during a coup attempt in 1934. In March 1938 German armies marched unopposed across the Austrian border and into the streets of Vienna. This so-called Anschluss made Austria a part of the German Reich, the new empire that Hitler had proclaimed as the worthy successor to the proud German states of the past.

In Britain and France, Hitler's actions inspired alarm but no action. In Czechoslovakia, however, a vulnerable government saw its turn coming. The German-speaking citizens of Czechoslovakia lived along the country's western frontiers with Germany, where Hitler's rise inspired a movement in support of annexation by Germany of this German-speaking Sudetenland. The government of France, obligated by treaty to protect Czechoslovakia from aggression, made a solemn vow to carry out its obligations and was seconded by Britain and Russia. Promising that the Sudetenland was the last annexation he would undertake, Hitler agreed to a meeting at the southern German city of Munich with Neville Chamberlain, prime minister of Britain, and Édouard Daladier, the premier of France (the Czech government was not allowed to send a delegate). With Mussolini at his side, Hitler angrily insisted on his claim, cowing his opponents and emerging with a treaty signed on September 29, 1938, which ceded the Sudetenland to the Third Reich. Chamberlain, who understood that war was coming and who was simply playing for time, returned to London and made a famous and ill-fated promise that he had achieved peace.

The Munich Agreement was followed by the invasion and annexation of the rest of Czechoslovakia in March 1939. Later, Germany seized the port of Memel, in Lithuania, while Italy invaded Albania. Piece by piece, Europe was falling under Axis domination while the non-Axis countries stood by, still unprepared for outright war.

World War II Begins

Hitler had pledged that the Sudetenland, and then Czecho-slovakia, would be the last of his conquests. But the easy victories and the growing Third Reich fired an ambition he had been harboring since the 1920s: the creation of lebensraum, or "living space," to the east for the burgeoning population of Germany. For centuries, this territory had been settled, shared, and contested by Germans and Slavs. The latest turn in this centuries-old struggle had taken place in 1919, when a large slice of Germany lying along the Baltic Sea had been turned over to Poland after World War I, an act that cut the German-ruled province of East Prussia from Germany proper. The port of Danzig and its German population had thus been placed under Polish sovereignty, a result that Hitler was now determined to overturn on the way to the annihilation of another neighboring country.

In August 1939 Hitler demanded the return of Danzig and the creation of a corridor linking Germany with East Prussia. In the meantime, his armies massed on the frontiers of Poland. Hitler realized that this next conquest would bring him to the border of the Soviet Union. When Neville Chamberlain announced that Britain would go to war in support of Poland, Hitler also realized that Germany was not prepared for war with Britain as well as the Soviet Red Army. While Germany strengthened the Siegfried Line, a series of fortifications facing the French border west of the Rhine River, a round of negotiations with Joseph Stalin, the Soviet leader, resulted in the Nazi-Soviet pact, an alliance that secretly promised both nations a share of the expected conquest of Poland.

Meanwhile, the leaders and people of Great Britain found themselves mired in a sense of helplessness and torpor even before the war had officially begun. Author Stephan Budiansky writes,

> Amid belated preparations for a war no longer unthinkable and impossible, but now become unthinkable and inevitable, the summer of 1939 for many in England took on a strange air of unreality, a slow and helpless descent into blackness. . . . [Future prime minister Winston] Churchill

railed against the British mien of unhurried imperturbability when a sense of urgency was what so obviously was required—urgency to press the negotiations with Russia to conclusion, urgency to get on with rearmament. Britain's ruling class continued "to take its weekends in the country," Churchill acidly observed, while "Hitler took his countries in the weekend." But Chamberlain did not like to be bothered with telephone calls after dinner or on weekends, and he saw no reason to alter his habits just because a war was about to start. . . . And so the world slid toward slaughter and calamity in an almost eerie calm.[1]

On September 1, 1939, Germany invaded Poland. The mobile German tank and armored divisions rolled across the Polish plains, encircling and defeating a Polish army that fought with outdated weapons and tactics. Germany's new blitzkrieg, or "lightning war," relied on the swift and independent movement of tank divisions behind enemy lines, working in cooperation with the Luftwaffe, or German air force. While dive-bombers and heavy bombers attacked railroads, factories, and cities, German infantry advanced through the scattered Polish defenses. The Soviet invasion of eastern Poland on September 17 forced the Polish army to fight on two fronts. The capital of Warsaw, the last pocket of resistance, fell on September 27.

Hitler and Stalin had conquered a large nation in less than a month, and the Allied powers, despite their promises to the contrary, had done nothing to prevent it. Britain and France had indeed declared war, but through the fall and winter they used only strong words to combat the actions of Germany and Italy. The Maginot Line, on the French side, and the Siegfried Line, on the German, remained quiet, but at sea, German battleships attacked merchant and naval ships of Britain and France. In the Allied countries, journalists and the public, in fear and in anger, used the term *phony war* to describe the inaction of their governments, hoping as well that the awful carnage of World War I could be avoided and Hitler, somehow, could be made to see reason.

Still not prepared for an invasion of France, Hitler ordered his armies to the north. Denmark and Norway were attacked on April 9, 1940. Although Denmark proved an easy conquest, Norway benefited from its mountainous and easily defended terrain. Britain and France sent troops, ships, and planes into Norway to fight the invasion, and the battle lasted a full two months before Germany succeeded in driving the Allies out of the country. In the meantime, on May 10, Germany invaded Belgium, Luxembourg, and the Netherlands. Luxembourg fell after a single day of fighting, and on May 28, the king of Belgium, Leopold III, surrendered himself and his army. While the German units drove to the coast of the English Channel, a half million Allied troops found themselves cut off and encircled. Instead of finishing off this last pocket of resistance in the Low Countries, however, Hitler ordered his army to halt twenty miles from the port of Dunkerque. This decision allowed 338,000 troops to escape the continent on a convoy of military transports, freighters, barges, and small private boats.

In Great Britain the population and the politicians realized that diplomacy had failed and that Germany had engaged them in all-out war. Neville Chamberlain, seen by most as an appeaser, was replaced by Winston Churchill, who had been warning his nation about Hitler for years and who, in his speeches, roused the British to resist. Churchill's rhetoric came at a crucial time, as the conquest of Western Europe had brought the German army to the southern shore of the English Channel, directly opposite England, and gave Hitler the chance to unleash the Luftwaffe against British cities and factories.

Expecting to repeat the experience of World War I, the French army began digging trenches in the valleys of the Somme and Aisne rivers in the northern plains of France. These defenses and the Maginot Line proved useless against the German blitzkrieg that began on June 5. Five days after the battle commenced, Benito Mussolini announced that Italy would begin fighting in cooperation with Germany. With the Italian army moving against southeastern France, the French army was split in two, allowing Germany a swift conquest in the north. The French capital of Paris fell on June 14, an event that convinced the French premier, Marshal Philippe Pétain, to surrender. On June 22, Hitler arrived at the forest of Compiegne, the site of the humiliating German surrender that took

Children sit among the remains of bombed buildings. For several months in 1940, the German air force raided London nearly every night.

place on November 11, 1918, and oversaw the formal French surrender and a revenge he had been seeking for more than twenty years. France was divided into a northern zone occupied by the German army and a southern zone under the control of a government established in the town of Vichy, under Pétain's leadership, which collaborated with the Nazi authorities. In the meantime, General Charles de Gaulle escaped to Britain, where a Free French government was formed and de Gaulle prepared for a return to the continent.

For several months Hitler had been preparing an invasion of Great Britain with a plan code-named Operation Sea Lion. Most members of the German military command hoped to avoid such a campaign, however, and convinced Hitler to begin with a bombing campaign that might accomplish a British surrender at lesser expense. The Battle of Britain began in July 1940 with the pilots of the Royal Air Force fighting the Luftwaffe to a stalemate that finally forced Germany to change its tactics in the fall, when daylight raids ended and night bombing commenced. For nine months, from September 1940 until May 1941, German bombers raided London nearly every night while Germany attempted to strike a bargain with Churchill that would allow Hitler to save face as well as the better part of the German air force. Their resistance stiffened by Churchill's rousing and determined rhetoric, the people of Britain watched as entire city blocks, monuments, factories, churches, and schools were destroyed by bombing and fire. By May 1941, however, the Luftwaffe had lost more than twenty-five hundred planes. German flights over Britain came nearly to a halt; the Battle of Britain was over, the first victory of any kind scored by the Allies against the Axis.

Italian Campaigns in Europe and Africa

By the initiative of Benito Mussolini, the war spread to southeastern Europe and North Africa at the same time Germany was attempting to bomb Great Britain into submission. Claiming sovereignty over Greece, Italy attacked from Albania but was defeated by determined resistance in the rugged mountains of Epirus in northern Greece. Although Hungary, Romania, and Bulgaria joined the Axis powers that fall as well, a German attack on Yugoslavia began a long and tough campaign between the German army and Yugoslav partisans, who succeeded in fighting the well-equipped and well-trained German army divisions to a stalemate. In April 1941 Germany's Balkan campaign ended with the capture of Athens and the surrender of the Greek government.

Across the Mediterranean, one Italian army had conquered Somaliland, a British colony lying east of Ethiopia; another one based along the Mediterranean coast of Libya had attacked British troops in Egypt. When the Italians were thrown back by a British army in February 1941, Hitler came to Mussolini's aid by sending a motorized army, known as the Afrika Korps, to North Africa. Fighting under the skilled leadership of General Erwin Rommel, the Afrika Korps drove the British out of Libya and as far east as the Nile River. The ultimate goal of Germany's North Africa campaign was the capture of oil fields in the Middle East that would allow Germany to draw on the most valuable resource of modern warfare.

On the Axis drawing board, this drive from Africa would

eventually be joined by an attack from the north, through the Caucasus Mountains, which lay within several republics of the Soviet Union. Germany and the Soviet Union were formally at peace, but the Nazi-Soviet pact, as both sides understood it, was simply a convenient arrangement that allowed both sides to go about conquering their neighbors without interference from the other side. In this spirit, Stalin ordered an invasion of Finland on November 30, 1939, a campaign that nearly resulted in the defeat of the Soviet army by a smaller but determined Finnish army and by bitterly cold weather. Finland surrendered in March 1940; that summer the Soviets invaded and absorbed the Baltic nations of Lithuania, Latvia, and Estonia, which provided a further territorial buffer against Germany.

His western front quiet and his southeastern fronts secure, Adolf Hitler made the fateful decision to attack the Soviet Union during the spring of 1941. Many historians have pointed to this campaign as the one decisive and fatal mistake that cost Germany the war. Michael Burleigh, in *The Third Reich: A New History,* describes the deep-seated fears of the East and of the Slavs as lying at the heart of Germany's eastern campaign:

> As was the case before Poland, a host of academic "experts" on the East (Ostforscher) . . . came out of the academic woodwork to proffer their detailed knowledge of Russia or the Soviet Union. . . . Inevitably, all of this information both reflected, or was combined with, longer-term perceptions and deeply entrenched stereotypes of the East in general and the Russians in particular. Nineteenth-century liberal and socialist Germans lived in dred of the knouts and sabres of the Tsars' semi-barbaric Cossack armies. . . . In sum, regardless of admiration for the stoic peasants as mediated by [Russian novelist Leo] Tolstoy, or the psychological sophistication of [author Fyodor] Dostoevsky, something at once inferior and threatening lurked out in the East.[2]

Operation Barbarossa, as it was code-named, began on June 22, 1941, with 150 German divisions attacking across a long front from the Baltic to the Black Sea. Caught completely off guard, the Red Army fell back, and German maneuvering resulted in the encirclement of several Soviet armies. The invasion threw Stalin himself into a state of shock and indecision that he was unable to overcome for two weeks. While Stalin gradually revived, Germany suffered from Hitler's own fatal weakness: overconfidence. Sure that Germany's blitzkrieg would make short work of the Red Army, the German leaders prepared themselves for a short, easy campaign in summer weather and an abject Soviet surrender, on the model of France, Denmark, and the Netherlands. At the same time, the Soviet government ordered the movement of entire factories to the east and to Siberia and prepared for the coming winter.

War in the Pacific

Japan's conquests in Asia had as their goal the establishment of the Greater East Asia Prosperity Sphere, a zone in which military occupation and exploitation of natural resources would contribute to greater Japanese prosperity. The French colony of Indochina fell to the Japanese in September 1940. By this time, Japan also controlled a large portion of mainland China after the initial invasions of the 1930s. The attack on Indochina, however, abruptly stopped trade in fuel, steel, and raw materials between the United States and Japan. Although the United States remained officially neutral in the war, the U.S. government was allying itself with the Allies through economic initiatives such as the Lend-Lease Program, which traded American war matériel for leases on bases in former British colonies in the Western Hemisphere.

Even though the United States supported Britain with words and with goods, a large segment of the U.S. population believed that their country should keep out of the war. The fight belonged to Europe, as had World War I, and Hitler seemed to pose no direct threat to the United States. The government of President Franklin Roosevelt worked against this opinion; military production was stepped up while a draft law was passed and the military reorganized itself on a wartime footing. As it happened, however, the decision to enter the war was made for the United States by the government of

Japan. By the fall of 1941, Japan was in the hands of a militaristic coterie headed by Lieutenant General Hideki Tojo. Angered and threatened by the embargoes and sanctions of the United States, Tojo ordered a preemptive strike on the U.S. naval and air bases on the island of Oahu in the Hawaiian Islands. The mission of the Japanese air force was to destroy so many planes and ships that the conquest of the eastern Pacific by Japan would proceed unopposed.

The attack on Pearl Harbor took place on the morning of December 7, 1941. On the following day, President Roosevelt asked a joint session of the U.S. Congress for a declaration of war on Japan. The declaration followed soon afterward, with only a single representative, Jeannette Rankin of Montana, dissenting. As carefully planned and well executed as the attack might have been, Japan had abruptly brought the United States, a major industrial and military power, into the war on the opposing side, a result that would bring about the destruction of the Axis. Ever since that day, historians have speculated freely about the circumstances surrounding Pearl Harbor, with many convinced that the attack was not a complete surprise to Roosevelt or his administration. After recounting a series of missed diplomatic signals and failed warnings to the Pearl Harbor commanders, historian John Toland summarized his findings as follows: "The comedy of errors on the sixth and seventh [of December] appears incredible. It only makes sense if it was a charade, and Roosevelt and the inner circle had known about the attack." [3]

The Turning Point

The next year proved to be the war's turning point. Germany's eastern advance stalled in the bitter Russian winter and stopped short of the Russian capital of Moscow, and in the south the German Sixth Army was cut off and encircled at the city of Stalingrad on the Volga River. The Allies invaded North Africa and attacked Rommel's Afrika Korps, defeating the Germans at the Battle of El Alamein in the Egyptian desert. With this victory, the Allies began a counteroffensive that drove Rommel out of Egypt and Libya altogether. On November 8, 1942, the armies of the United States and the Allies landed in Algeria and

Morocco in Operation Torch. The attacks from east and west would, in May 1943, drive the Afrika Korps entirely out of Africa. This event stopped Germany's plan of conquest in the Middle East, where British troops installed governments friendly to the Allies in Iran, Iraq, Syria, and Lebanon.

The Allies used Operation Torch as a dress rehearsal for the coming task of landing in and fighting for Nazi-held territory in Europe. Italy and Mussolini were targeted as the weakest link in the Axis fortress of Europe. On July 10, 1943, the Allies landed in Sicily. This first fighting on Italian soil turned many Italians against Mussolini, who fell from power and was imprisoned. In September, British and American armies landed on the Italian peninsula. Italy abandoned the Axis and officially declared war on Germany in October. Over the next six months, a German army fought desperately to hold the mountains of central Italy against a relentless Allied advance.

Allied commanders had been planning an invasion of northern Europe since shortly after the United States had entered the war. Roosevelt, Churchill, and Stalin came to an important mutual understanding: Germany, as the most powerful Axis power, must be defeated first. An attack in France would open up a new front, forcing Germany to divide its forces and fight in Russia and western Europe. Realizing this, Hitler ordered the reinforcement of coastal defenses along the Atlantic Ocean, the English Channel, and the North Sea. For the Allies, a dress rehearsal was needed and was carried out on the coastal French town of Dieppe in August 1942. This raid on a heavily defended coastline presaged the much larger invasion of Normandy that took place on June 6, 1944. The "D day" landings accomplished their goal after several weeks of hard fighting in northwestern France. German armies fell back while Hitler deployed a secret weapon that he hoped would finally force the Allies into an armistice: the V-1 "buzz bomb" and the V-2 missile were launched against Great Britain.

A New War in the Pacific

At the beginning of 1942, the Japanese army held eastern Asia from Manchuria to the Dutch East Indies. The attack on

Pearl Harbor marked the start of a surprise campaign against U.S. bases in the central Pacific, the Philippines, Hong Kong, and the stronghold of Singapore at the tip of the Malay Peninsula. With the U.S. Navy reeling, the Japanese pressed their advantage by sending a fleet of aircraft carriers through the northern Pacific Ocean, in the direction of Hawaii and the west coast of the United States. The fleet intended to destroy the American carriers that had been out of port at the time of the Pearl Harbor attack and convince the United States that a reconquest of the eastern Pacific from Japan would be too costly.

On June 4, 1942, aircraft from the Japanese carriers began bombing Midway Island, one thousand miles northwest of Hawaii. Prepared for this battle with decoded messages and orders issued by the Japanese military, the United States counterattacked with a powerful force of aircraft carriers. In two days, four Japanese carriers were sunk and the better part of the Japanese air force was destroyed. The Battle of Midway ended the Japanese threat to the United States and opened the Pacific theater to offensive operations by the United States. Over the next three years, beginning with Guadalcanal in the Solomon Islands in August 1942, the United States carried out an amphibious war against Japanese-held islands and coastal strongholds in the Pacific. This was a new kind of war at sea, in which ships cooperated with planes and infantry units in carefully coordinated amphibious invasions. The ultimate objective was to seize an island base close enough to Japan to allow a direct attack on Japan's "home islands." The Gilbert Islands were seized in late 1943; in the next year the United States also landed in the Marshall Islands and Guam while a southern force worked up the coast of New Guinea and attacked the Philippines. An immense U.S. air and naval force contested for control of the straits, bays, and islands of the Philippines in what became known as the Battle of Leyte Gulf. The largest naval battle in history, Leyte Gulf resulted in the sinking of twenty-six major Japanese ships and the recapture of the Philippine Islands.

Its naval and air forces crippled by this defeat, Japan could offer only suicidal air attacks and ground defense in resistance to the U.S. advance. The island of Iwo Jima fell on March 16, 1945, after twenty-six days of savage fighting between American marines and Japanese defenders protected by a network of fortified bunkers and caves. In the spring of 1945 the island of Okinawa was captured, setting the stage for the final act of the Pacific war: an invasion of Japan itself, planned for November 1945.

In Europe, the Allies were advancing on Hitler from east and west. German conquests—the Netherlands, Denmark, Norway, and Greece—fell one by one to the Allies while German troops retreated into Germany proper. A bombing campaign carried out by British and American high-level bombers destroyed German cities and industry, making it impossible for Germany to reinforce its depleted military. The capture of Berlin, Germany's capital, in late April finally brought Adolf Hitler to the realization that the war was lost. Hitler committed suicide on April 30, 1945; one week later Germany formally surrendered.

The surrender of Germany left Japan as the only Axis power standing, yet the Japanese government would not accept unconditional surrender. The attacks on the islands of the Pacific had coincided with a relentless bombing campaign carried out by the United States against Japan's capital, Tokyo, a city largely made of fragile wood homes. The bombing resulted in massive firestorms that killed thousands of people. In Japan and in Europe, Allied commanders saw aerial bombing of civilian homes and industry targets as the most effective method of fighting the war—a view fraught with moral dilemmas that historians have debated since the war ended. As Richard Overy explains in *Why the Allies Won,*

> Bombing has occasioned a chorus of moral disapproval. Yet to understand what bombing achieved it is necessary, though agonisingly difficult, to lay aside the moral issue. Its strategic merits or limitations are distinct from its ethical implications, however closely entwined they have become in the contemporary debate. . . . Bombing did reduce the overall level of western casualties in Europe and in the Far East, by weakening German resistance and by knocking Japan out of the war before invasion. Bombing also permitted Britain and the United States to bring their consider-

able economic and scientific power to bear on the contest. That suited the preferences of the west, which did not want to place a much higher physical strain on their populations.[4]

Convinced that the only alternative would be a ground invasion of Japan resulting in horrendous casualties, President Harry Truman ordered atomic bombs to be dropped on Hiroshima and Nagasaki in August, 1945. Two entire cities were destroyed and more than one hundred thousand people were killed. Aboard the U.S. battleship *Missouri* at anchor in Tokyo Bay, the Japanese signed a formal surrender on September 2, 1945.

World War II had ended after six years and a measureless loss in human life and property. The effects of the war can still be felt throughout the world. It began with a remaking of the political landscape of Great Britain and the European continent, as described by historian Mark Mazower:

> Suspect as the notion may seem to revisionists today, social revolution hardly seems too strong a term to describe the dramatic changes wrought by the war both in Britain and in occupied Europe. Wartime dislocation and chaos—some sixty million changes of address were registered in Britain alone during the war—collapsed the social distances upon which the rigid pre-war class systems of Europe had rested. The impact of bombing, together with systematic evacuations and the mass panics and flight of millions of people . . . brought classes and communities together which had formerly remained in ignorance of one another.[5]

The occupation of Germany by the Allies in 1945 divided the country into Eastern and Western zones, a division that would last until the early 1990s. The mighty army and navy of Japan disappeared, to be replaced by a purely defensive force and allowing Japan to develop an economy that grew into one of the world's most powerful during the late twentieth century. The atomic weapons of Hiroshima and Nagasaki were further refined and developed into intercontinental ballistic missiles that threatened the existence of the Soviet Union and the United States, two Allied countries that were turned into political and economic rivals by the postwar Cold

War, which spawned smaller wars in Korea and Vietnam.

World War II represented the end of an era of all-out ground warfare in which massive armies attacked, held, and moved across huge swaths of enemy territory. During the last half of the twentieth century, aerial bombing was replacing ground offensives, and the threat of atomic annihilation was inhibiting military posturing among the world's major powers. World War II also represented the end of traditional means of propagandizing war. The terrible events were relayed by print media and by the radio, not by television, and the spoken words of political leaders proved the most effective weapon of all in mobilizing civilians and soldiers to sacrifice for a common cause. Both the Axis and Allied leaders understood the leading role of propaganda and persuasion, and these leaders took great care to strike the desired effect with their public speeches. During the twenty-first century, in which images commonly overwhelm speech, political leaders may read the powerful phrases of Hitler, Mussolini, Roosevelt, Churchill, and other figures with nostalgia for a time when the spoken word held a commanding role in the deeds and misdeeds of the world's nations.

Notes

1. Stephen Budiansky, *Battle of Wits: The Complete Story of Codebreaking in World War II.* New York: Free, 2000, pp. 92–93.

2. Michael Burleigh, *The Third Reich: A New History.* New York: Hill and Wang, 2000, p. 490.

3. John Toland, *Infamy: Pearl Harbor and Its Aftermath.* Garden City, NY: Doubleday, 1982, p. 321.

4. Richard Overy, *Why the Allies Won.* New York: W.W. Norton, 1995, p. 128.

5. Mark Mazower, *Dark Continent: Europe's Twentieth Century.* New York: Alfred A. Knopf, 1999, p. 185.

CHAPTER ONE

**GREAT
SPEECHES
IN
HISTORY**

Prelude
to War

Mussolini's Italy Conquers Ethiopia

Haile Selassie

Crowned emperor of Ethiopia in 1930, Haile Selassie ener-getically undertook the modernization of his country, which was recognized by the European powers as indepen-dent and which had been a member of the League of Na-tions since 1924. Unfortunately for Ethiopia, Italian dicta-tor Benito Mussolini had designs of conquest in Africa. Seeking a victory that would make his nation the equal of the other "great powers" of Europe and bring his regime prestige at home, Mussolini used the small Italian colony of Eritrea, lying on Ethiopia's northern border, as a base.

In December 1934 Mussolini staged a confrontation known as the Wal Wal incident, a skirmish over an iso-lated desert outpost, just inside the Ethiopian border, in which British, Ethiopian, and Italian units suffered sev-eral hundred casualties. Mussolini used the Wal Wal inci-dent as a pretext to invade Ethiopia in October 1935. The League of Nations—founded after World War I to prevent such acts of war—condemned the invasion. But its members took no action to pressure Italy to withdraw or to preserve Ethiopia's sovereignty. Selassie fled into ex-ile on May 2, 1936. On June 30 he went to Geneva to confront the League of Nations and condemn the inva-sion of his country.

In his speech, Selassie gives details of Italian atroci-ties, including the use of poison gas, an act directly con-trary to international treaties signed during the 1920s. Although his appeal gained widespread sympathy, it pro-voked no action, and Britain and France eventually rec-

Excerpted from Haile Selassie's speech delivered to the League of Nations, June 30, 1936.

ognized Italy's claims to Ethiopia. A few months after this speech, Italy and Germany concluded the pact that established the Axis alliance of fascist nations.

I, Haile Selassie I, Emperor of Ethiopia, am here today to claim that justice which is due to my people, and the assistance promised to it eight months ago, when fifty nations asserted that aggression had been committed in violation of international treaties. There is no precedent for a Head of State himself speaking in this assembly. But there is also no precedent for a people being victim of such injustice and being at present threatened by abandonment to its aggressor. Also, there has never before been an example of any Government proceeding to the systematic extermination of a nation by barbarous means, in violation of the most solemn promises made by the nations of the earth that there should not be used against innocent human beings the terrible poison of harmful gases. It is to defend a people struggling for its age-old independence that the head of the Ethiopian Empire has come to Geneva to fulfil this supreme duty, after having himself fought at the head of his armies.

I pray to Almighty God that He may spare nations the terrible sufferings that have just been inflicted on my people, and of which the chiefs who accompany me here have been the horrified witnesses.

It is my duty to inform the Governments assembled in Geneva, responsible as they are for the lives of millions of men, women and children, of the deadly peril which threatens them, by describing to them the fate which has been suffered by Ethiopia.

It is not only upon warriors that the Italian Government has made war. It has above all attacked populations far removed from hostilities, in order to terrorize and exterminate them.

At the beginning, towards the end of 1935, Italian aircraft hurled upon my armies bombs of tear-gas. Their effects were but slight. The soldiers learned to scatter, waiting until the wind had rapidly dispersed the poisonous gases. The Italian aircraft then resorted to mustard gas. Barrels of liquid were hurled upon armed groups. But this means also was not effective; the liquid affected only a few soldiers, and barrels upon the ground were themselves a warning to troops and to the population of the danger.

It was at the time when the operations for the encircling of Makalle were taking place that the Italian command, fearing a rout, followed the procedure which it is now my duty to denounce to the world. Special sprayers were installed on board aircraft so that they could vaporize, over vast areas of territory, a fine, death-dealing rain. Groups of nine, fifteen, eighteen aircraft followed one another so that the fog issuing from them formed a continuous sheet. It was thus that, as from the end of January, 1936, soldiers, women, children, cattle, rivers, lakes and pastures were drenched continually with this deadly rain. In order to kill off systematically all living creatures, in order to more surely poison waters and pastures, the Italian command made its aircraft pass over and over again. That was its chief method of warfare.

The very refinement of barbarism consisted in carrying ravage and terror into the most densely populated parts of the territory, the points farthest removed from the scene of hostilities. The object was to scatter fear and death over a great part of the Ethiopian territory.

These fearful tactics succeeded. Men and animals succumbed. The deadly rain that fell from the aircraft made all those whom it touched fly shrieking with pain. All those who drank the poisoned water or ate the infected food also succumbed in dreadful suffering. In tens of thousands, the victims of the Italian mustard gas fell. It is in order to denounce to the civilized world the tortures inflicted upon the Ethiopian people that I resolved to come to Geneva. None other than myself and my brave companions in arms could bring the League of Nations the undeniable proof. The appeals of my delegates addressed to the League of Nations had remained without any answer; my delegates had not been witnesses. That is why I decided to come myself to bear witness against the crime perpetrated against my people and give Europe a warning of the doom that awaits it, if it should bow before the accomplished fact.

Treaties of Friendship with Italy

Is it necessary to remind the Assembly of the various stages of the Ethiopian drama? For 20 years past, either as Heir Apparent, Regent of the Empire, or as Emperor, I have never ceased to use all my efforts to bring my country the benefits of civilization, and in particular to establish relations of good neighbourliness with adjacent powers. In particular I succeeded in concluding with Italy the Treaty of Friendship of 1928, which absolutely prohibited the resort, under any pretext whatsoever, to force of arms, substituting for force and pressure the conciliation and arbitration on which civilized nations have based international order.

In its report of October 5th, 1935, the Committee of Thirteen recognized my effort and the results that I had achieved. The Governments thought that the entry of Ethiopia into the League, whilst giving that country a new guarantee for the maintenance of her territorial integrity and independence, would help her to reach a higher level of civilization. It does not seem that in Ethiopia today there is more disorder and insecurity than in 1923. On the contrary, the country is more united and the central power is better obeyed.

I should have procured still greater results for my people if obstacles of every kind had not been put in the way by the Italian Government, the Government which stirred up revolt and armed the rebels. Indeed the Rome Government, as it has today openly proclaimed, has never ceased to prepare for the conquest of Ethiopia. The Treaties of Friendship it signed with me were not sincere; their only object was to hide its real intention from me. The Italian Government asserts that for 14 years it has been preparing for its present conquest. It therefore recognizes today that when it supported the admission of Ethiopia to the League of Nations in 1923, when it concluded the Treaty of Friendship in 1928, when it signed the Pact of Paris outlawing war, it was deceiving the whole world. The Ethiopian Government was, in these solemn treaties, given additional guarantees of security which would enable it to achieve further progress along the specific path of reform on which it had set its feet, and to which it was devoting all its strength and all its heart.

Italy's Provocation to War

The Wal-Wal [Welwel] incident, in December, 1934, came as a thunderbolt to me. The Italian provocation was obvious and I did not hesitate to appeal to the League of Nations. I invoked the provisions of the treaty of 1928, the principles of the Covenant; I urged the procedure of conciliation and arbitration. Unhappily for Ethiopia this was the time when a certain Government considered that the European situation made it imperative at all costs to obtain the friendship of Italy. The price paid was the abandonment of Ethiopian independence to the greed of the Italian Government. This secret agreement, contrary to the obligations of the Covenant, has exerted a great influence over the course of events. Ethiopia and the whole world have suffered and are still suffering today its disastrous consequences.

This first violation of the Covenant was followed by many others. Feeling itself encouraged in its policy against Ethiopia, the Rome Government feverishly made war preparations, thinking that the concerted pressure which was beginning to be exerted on the Ethiopian Government, might perhaps not overcome the resistance of my people to Italian domination. The time had to come, thus all sorts of difficulties were placed in the way with a view to breaking up the procedure of conciliation and arbitration. All kinds of obstacles were placed in the way of that procedure. Governments tried to prevent the Ethiopian Government from finding arbitrators amongst their nationals: when once the arbitral tribunal was set up pressure was exercised so that an award favourable to Italy should be given.

All this was in vain: the arbitrators, two of whom were Italian officials, were forced to recognize unanimously that in the Wal-Wal incident, as in the subsequent incidents, no international responsibility was to be attributed to Ethiopia.

Following on this award, the Ethiopian Government sincerely thought that an era of friendly relations might be opened with Italy. I loyally offered my hand to the Roman Government.

The Assembly was informed by the report of the Committee of Thirteen, dated October 5th, 1935, of the details of the events which occurred after the month of December, 1934, and up to October 3rd, 1935.

The Inaction of the League of Nations

It will be sufficient if I quote a few of the conclusions of that report: "The Italian memorandum (containing the complaints made by Italy) was laid on the Council table on September 4th, 1935, whereas Ethiopia's first appeal to the Council had been made on December 14th, 1934. In the interval between these two dates, the Italian Government opposed the consideration of the question by the Council on the ground that the only appropriate procedure was that provided for in the Italo-Ethiopian Treaty of 1928. Throughout the whole of that period, moreover, the despatch of Italian troops to East Africa was proceeding. These shipments of troops were represented to the Council by the Italian Government as necessary for the defense of its colonies menaced by Ethiopia's preparations. Ethiopia, on the contrary, drew attention to the official pronouncements made in Italy which, in its opinion, left no doubt "as to the hostile intentions of the Italian Government." From the outset of the dispute, the Ethiopian Government has sought a settlement by peaceful means. It has appealed to the procedures of the Covenant. The Italian Government desiring to keep strictly to the procedures of the Italo-Ethiopian Treaty of 1928, the Ethiopian Government assented. It invariably stated that it would faithfully carry out the arbitral award even if the decision went against it. It agreed that the question of the ownership of Wal-Wal should not be dealt with by the arbitrators, because the Italian Government would not agree to such a course. It asked the Council to despatch neutral observers and offered to lend itself to any enquiries upon which the Council might decide.

Once the Wal-Wal dispute had been settled by arbitration, however, the Italian Government submitted its detailed memorandum to the Council in support of its claim to liberty of action. It asserted that a case like that of Ethiopia cannot be settled by the means provided by the Covenant.

It stated that, "since this question affects vital interest and is of primary importance to Italian security and civilization" it "would be failing in its most elementary duty, did it not cease once and for all to place any confidence in Ethiopia, reserving full liberty to adopt any measures that may become necessary to ensure the safety of its colonies and to safeguard its own interests."

Those are the terms of the report of the Committee of Thirteen. The Council and the Assembly unanimously adopted the conclusion that the Italian Government had violated the Covenant and was in a state of aggression. I did not hesitate to declare that I did not wish for war, that it was imposed upon me, and I should struggle solely for the independence and integrity of my people, and that in that struggle I was the defender of the cause of all small States exposed to the greed of a powerful neighbour.

In October, 1935, the 52 nations who are listening to me today gave me an assurance that the aggressor would not triumph, that the resources of the Covenant would be employed in order to ensure the reign of right and the failure of violence.

I ask the fifty-two nations not to forget today the policy upon which they embarked eight months ago, and on faith of which I directed the resistance of my people against the aggressor whom they had denounced to the world. Despite the inferiority of my weapons, the complete lack of aircraft, artillery, munitions, hospital services, my confidence in the League was absolute. I thought it to be impossible that fifty-two nations, including the most powerful in the world, should be successfully opposed by a single aggressor. Counting on the faith due to treaties, I had made no preparation for war, and that is the case with certain small countries in Europe.

When the danger became more urgent, being aware of my responsibilities towards my people, during the first six months of 1935 I tried to acquire armaments. Many Governments proclaimed an embargo to prevent my doing so, whereas the Italian Government through the Suez Canal, was given all facilities for transporting without cessation and without protest, troops, arms, and munitions.

On October 3rd, 1935, the Italian troops invaded my territory. A few hours later only I decreed general mobilization. In my desire to maintain peace I had, following the example of a great country in Europe on the eve of the Great War,

caused my troops to withdraw thirty kilometres so as to remove any pretext of provocation.

War then took place in the atrocious conditions which I
have laid before the Assembly. In that unequal struggle between a Government commanding more than forty-two million inhabitants, having at its disposal financial, industrial
and technical means which enabled it to create unlimited
quantities of the most death-dealing weapons, and, on the
other hand, a small people of twelve million inhabitants,
without arms, without resources having on its side only the
justice of its own cause and the promise of the League of Nations. What real assistance was given to Ethiopia by the fifty-
two nations who had declared the Rome Government guilty
of a breach of the Covenant and had undertaken to prevent
the triumph of the aggressor? Has each of the . . . Members,
as it was its duty to do in virtue of its signature appended to
Article 15 of the Covenant, considered the aggressor as having committed an act of war personally directed against itself? I had placed all my hopes in the execution of these undertakings. My confidence had been confirmed by the
repeated declarations made in the Council to the effect that
aggression must not be rewarded, and that force would end
by being compelled to bow before right.

In December, 1935, the Council made it quite clear that
its feelings were in harmony with those of hundreds of millions of people who, in all parts of the world, had protested
against the proposal to dismember Ethiopia. It was constantly repeated that there was not merely a conflict between
the Italian Government and the League of Nations, and that
is why I personally refused all proposals to my personal advantage made to me by the Italian Government, if only I
would betray my people and the Covenant of the League of
Nations. I was defending the cause of all small peoples who
are threatened with aggression.

What have become of the promises made to me as long
ago as October, 1935? I noted with grief, but without surprise that three Powers considered their undertakings under
the Covenant as absolutely of no value. Their connections
with Italy impelled them to refuse to take any measures
whatsoever in order to stop Italian aggression. On the con-

trary, it was a profound disappointment to me to learn the attitude of a certain Government which, whilst ever protesting its scrupulous attachment to the Covenant, has tirelessly used all its efforts to prevent its observance. As soon as any measure which was likely to be rapidly effective was proposed, various pretexts were devised in order to postpone even consideration of the measure. Did the secret agreements of January, 1935, provide for this tireless obstruction?

The Ethiopian Government never expected other Governments to shed their soldiers' blood to defend the Covenant when their own immediately personal interests were not at stake. Ethiopian warriors asked only for means to defend themselves. On many occasions I have asked for financial assistance for the purchase of arms. That assistance has been constantly refused me. What, then, in practice, is the meaning of Article 16 of the Covenant and of collective security?

The Ethiopian Government's use of the railway from Djibouti to Addis Ababa was in practice a hazardous transport of arms intended for the Ethiopian forces. At the present moment this is the chief, if not the only means of supply of the Italian armies of occupation. The rules of neutrality should have prohibited transports intended for Italian forces, but there is not even neutrality since Article 16 lays upon every . . . Member of the League the duty not to remain a neutral but to come to the aid not of the aggressor but of the victim of aggression. Has the Covenant been respected? Is it today being respected?

Finally a statement has just been made in their Parliaments by the Governments of certain Powers, amongst them the most influential members of the League of Nations, that since the aggressor has succeeded in occupying a large part of Ethiopian territory they propose not to continue the application of any economic and financial measures that may have been decided upon against the Italian Government.

The Issue of Collective Security

These are the circumstances in which at the request of the Argentine Government, the Assembly of the League of Nations meets to consider the situation created by Italian aggression.

I assert that the problem submitted to the Assembly today is a much wider one. It is not merely a question of the settlement of Italian aggression.

It is collective security: it is the very existence of the League of Nations. It is the confidence that each State is to place in international treaties. It is the value of promises made to small States that their integrity and their independence shall be respected and ensured. It is the principle of the equality of States on the one hand, or otherwise the obligation laid upon small Powers to accept the bonds of vassalship. In a word, it is international morality that is at stake. Have the signatures appended to a Treaty value only in so far as the signatory Powers have a personal, direct and immediate interest involved?

No subtlety can change the problem or shift the grounds of the discussion. It is in all sincerity that I submit these considerations to the Assembly. At a time when my people are threatened with extermination, when the support of the League may ward off the final blow, may I be allowed to speak with complete frankness, without reticence, in all directness such as is demanded by the rule of equality as between all . . . Members of the League?

Apart from the Kingdom of the Lord there is not on this earth any nation that is superior to any other. Should it happen that a strong Government finds it may with impunity destroy a weak people, then the hour strikes for that weak people to appeal to the League of Nations to give its judgment in all freedom. God and history will remember your judgment.

I have heard it asserted that the inadequate sanctions already applied have not achieved their object. At no time, and under no circumstances could sanctions that were intentionally inadequate, intentionally badly applied, stop an aggressor. This is not a case of the impossibility of stopping an aggressor but of the refusal to stop an aggressor. When Ethiopia requested and requests that she should be given financial assistance, was that a measure which it was impossible to apply whereas financial assistance of the League has been granted, even in times of peace, to two countries and exactly to two countries who have refused to apply sanctions against the aggressor?

Faced by numerous violations by the Italian Government

of all international treaties that prohibit resort to arms, and the use of barbarous methods of warfare, it is my painful duty to note that the initiative has today been taken with a view to raising sanctions. Does this initiative not mean in practice the abandonment of Ethiopia to the aggressor? On the very eve of the day when I was about to attempt a supreme effort in the defense of my people before this Assembly does not this initiative deprive Ethiopia of one of her last chances to succeed in obtaining the support and guarantee of . . . Members? Is that the guidance the League of Nations and each of the . . . Members are entitled to expect from the great Powers when they assert their right and their duty to guide the action of the League? Placed by the aggressor face to face with the accomplished fact, are States going to set up the terrible precedent of bowing before force? Your Assembly will doubtless have laid before it proposals for the reform of the Covenant and for rendering more effective the guarantee of collective security. Is it the Covenant that needs reform? What undertakings can have any value if the will to keep them is lacking? It is international morality which is at stake and not the Articles of the Covenant. On behalf of the Ethiopian people, a member of the League of Nations, I request the Assembly to take all measures proper to ensure respect for the Covenant. I renew my protest against the violations of treaties of which the Ethiopian people has been the victim. I declare in the face of the whole world that the Emperor, the Government and the people of Ethiopia will not bow before force; that they maintain their claims that they will use all means in their power to ensure the triumph of right and the respect of the Covenant.

I ask the fifty-two nations, who have given the Ethiopian people a promise to help them in their resistance to the aggressor, what are they willing to do for Ethiopia? And the great Powers who have promised the guarantee of collective security to small States on whom weighs the threat that they may one day suffer the fate of Ethiopia, I ask what measures do you intend to take? Representatives of the World, I have come to Geneva to discharge in your midst the most painful of the duties of the head of a State. What reply shall I have to take back to my people?

Britain Must Fight

Neville Chamberlain

In March 1938 German chancellor Adolf Hitler annexed his southern neighbor, Austria. In September he moved German forces to the frontier with Czechoslovakia, fomenting a crisis and demanding the concession of the Sudetenland, a region of German-speaking Czechs.

Hitler's aggression threw the European powers into turmoil. There seemed to be no diplomatic solution. The League of Nations had done nothing to stop the Japanese invasion of Manchuria in 1931, nor the Italian conquest of Ethiopia in 1936. The leaders of Britain and France realized that only war could stop Hitler, but they did not believe that their countries were ready to match Germany's military. As a result, French prime minister Édouard Daladier and British prime minister Neville Chamberlain persuaded Edvard Beneš, the president of Czechoslovakia, to give up the Sudetenland, although such a move would leave Czechoslovakia defenseless against an invasion of the rest of its territory. On September 29, 1938, the leaders of France, Britain, Italy, and Germany met in Munich, Germany, to formally arrange the surrender. The agreement that resulted allowed Germany to annex the Sudetenland.

Convinced that Britain was not prepared for a war, Chamberlain intended to buy time so that his country could rearm. When he returned to England on September 30, he stepped from the plane, waved the agreement in the air, and delivered the following speech:

We, the German Fuhrer and Chancellor, and the British Prime Minister, have had a further meeting today and are

---

Excerpted from Neville Chamberlain's speech in England, September 1, 1939.

agreed in recognizing that the question of Anglo-German relations is of the first importance for our two countries and for Europe.

We regard the agreement signed last night and the Anglo-German Naval Agreement as symbolic of the desire of our two peoples never to go to war with one another again.

We are resolved that the method of consultation shall be the method adopted to deal with any other questions that may concern our two countries, and we are determined to continue our efforts to remove possible sources of difference, and thus to continue to assure the peace of Europe.

My good friends, this is the second time in our history that there has come back from Germany to Downing Street peace with honor. I believe it is peace in our time.

Unfortunately, Chamberlain was to be disappointed. In March 1939 Hitler marched his troops into the rest of Czechoslovakia and occupied the capital of Prague. On September 1, 1939, Germany attacked Poland, marking the traditional start of World War II. A few hours after this attack, in a speech to the British Parliament, Chamberlain admitted that his negotiated truce with Germany had failed and declared that the British government finally stood ready to fight.

I do not propose to say many words tonight. The time has come when action rather than speech is required. Eighteen months ago in this House I prayed that the responsibility might not fall upon me to ask this country to accept the awful arbitrament of war. I fear that I may not be able to avoid that responsibility.

But, at any rate, I cannot wish for conditions in which such a burden should fall upon me in which I should feel clearer than I do today as to where my duty lies.

No man can say that the Government could have done more to try to keep open the way for an honorable and equitable settlement of the dispute between Germany and Poland.

Nor have we neglected any means of making it crystal clear to the German Government that if they insisted on using force again in the manner in which they had used it in the past we were resolved to oppose them by force.

Now that all the relevant documents are being made public we shall stand at the bar of history knowing that the responsibility for this terrible catastrophe lies on the shoulders of one man, the German Chancellor [Adolf Hitler], who has not hesitated to plunge the world into misery in order to serve his own senseless ambitions. . . .

Only last night the Polish Ambassador did see the German Foreign Secretary, Herr [Joachim] von Ribbentrop. Once again he expressed to him what, indeed, the Polish Government had already said publicly, that they were willing to negotiate with Germany about their disputes on an equal basis.

What was the reply of the German Government? The reply was that without another word the German troops crossed the Polish frontier this morning at dawn and are since reported to be bombing open towns. In these circumstances there is only one course open to us.

His Majesty's Ambassador in Berlin and the French Ambassador have been instructed to hand to the German Government the following document:

> Early this morning the German Chancellor issued a proclamation to the German Army which indicated that he was about to attack Poland. Information which has reached His Majesty's Government in the United Kingdom and the French Government indicates that attacks upon Polish towns are proceeding. In these circumstances it appears to the Governments of the United Kingdom and France that by their action the German Government have created conditions, namely, an aggressive act of force against Poland threatening the independence of Poland, which call for the implementation by the Government of the United Kingdom and France of the undertaking to Poland to come to her assistance. I am accordingly to inform your Excellency that unless the German Government are prepared to give His Majesty's Government satisfactory assurances that the German Government have suspended all aggressive action against Poland and are prepared promptly to withdraw

their forces from Polish territory, His Majesty's Government in the United Kingdom will without hesitation fulfill their obligations to Poland.

If a reply to this last warning is unfavorable, and I do not suggest that it is likely to be otherwise, His Majesty's Ambassador is instructed to ask for his passports. In that case we are ready.

Yesterday, we took further steps towards the completion of our defensive preparation. This morning we ordered complete mobilization of the whole of the Royal Navy, Army and Royal Air Force. We have also taken a number of other measures, both at home and abroad, which the House will not perhaps expect me to specify in detail. Briefly, they represent the final steps in accordance with pre-arranged plans. These last can be put into force rapidly, and are of such a nature that they can be deferred until war seems inevitable. Steps have also been taken under the powers conferred by the House last week to safeguard the position in regard to stocks of commodities of various kinds.

Preparation for War

The thoughts of many of us must at this moment inevitably be turning back to 1914, and to a comparison of our position now with that which existed then. How do we stand this time? The answer is that all three Services are ready, and that the situation in all directions is far more favorable and reassuring than in 1914, while behind the fighting Services we have built up a vast organization of Civil Defense under our scheme of Air Raid Precautions.

As regards the immediate manpower requirements, the Royal Navy, the Army and the Air Force are in the fortunate position of having almost as many men as they can conveniently handle at this moment. There are, however, certain categories of service in which men are immediately required, both for Military and Civil Defense. These will be announced in detail through the press and the BBC.

The main and most satisfactory point to observe is that there is today no need to make an appeal in a general way for recruits such as was issued by [secretary of state for war] Lord

[Horatio] Kitchener 25 years ago. That appeal has been anticipated by many months, and the men are already available. So much for the immediate present. Now we must look to the future. It is essential in the face of the tremendous task which confronts us, more especially in view of our past experiences in this matter, to organize our manpower this time upon as methodical, equitable and economical a basis as possible.

We, therefore, propose immediately to introduce legislation directed to that end. A Bill will be laid before you which for all practical purposes will amount to an expansion of the Military Training Act. Under its operation all fit men between the ages of 18 and 41 will be rendered liable to military service if and when called upon. It is not intended at the outset that any considerable number of men other than those already liable shall be called up, and steps will be taken to ensure that the manpower essentially required by industry shall not be taken away.

There is one other allusion which I should like to make before I end my speech, and that is to record my satisfaction of His Majesty's Government, that throughout these last days of crisis [Italian dictator] Signor [Benito] Mussolini also has been doing his best to reach a solution. It now only remains for us to set our teeth and to enter upon this struggle, which we ourselves earnestly endeavored to avoid, with determination to see it through to the end.

We shall enter it with a clear conscience, with the support of the Dominions and the British Empire, and the moral approval of the greater part of the world.

We have no quarrel with the German people, except that they allow themselves to be governed by a Nazi Government. As long as that Government exists and pursues the methods it has so persistently followed during the last two years, there will be no peace in Europe. We shall merely pass from one crisis to another, and see one country after another attacked by methods which have now become familiar to us in their sickening technique.

We are resolved that these methods must come to an end. If out of the struggle we again re-establish in the world the rules of good faith and the renunciation of force, why, then even the sacrifices that will be entailed upon us will find their fullest justification.

The Attack on China

Chiang Kai-shek

Eager to establish its hegemony in Asia and led by a militaristic cabinet of ministers, Japan claimed most of eastern Asia—including mainland China, Korea, Southeast Asia, and the archipelagos lying between the mainland and Australia—as its proper sphere of influence. The Japanese had begun their conquest by invading Manchuria, a resource-rich region of northern China, in 1931. By 1938 most of China was under occupation by the Japanese, whose government was aligning itself with the Axis powers of Germany and Italy.

The Chinese leaders fled their capitals at Beijing and Nanjing to the interior city of Chongqing. On December 22, 1938, the Japanese prime minister, Prince Fumimaro Konoe, laid down three conditions for a settlement, which would have established permanent Japanese dominance of the Chinese government and economy. In response, Chiang Kai-shek, the head of the Chinese government in exile, gave the following speech to a meeting of the Kuomintang (Chinese nationalist army) at Chongqing.

The year and a half's war has laid for us a solid foundation for national regeneration. We fear no problems, nor are we concerned over impending dangers. We merely lament the fate of Japan, the present status of which was brought about by the hard efforts and sacrifices of her reformist patriots. Today, her people are powerless,

Excerpted fron Chiang Kai-shek's speech to the Kuomintang at Chongqing, December 26, 1938.

her throne without prerogative, and her politicians without integrity and knowledge, thus allowing a few hot-headed young militarists to do as they please. They are sapping Japan's national strength, shaking her national foundations and advancing savagely on the infamous road of self-seeking at the expense of others. In the eyes of these young Japanese militarists, China does not exist, nor do the other countries of the world. They have regard neither for discipline, nor for law, nor yet for their own government. Guided by their greed, cruelty, and violence, they do as they please. If such conduct be allowed to continue, the future of Japan is indeed full of danger. Although we are sworn enemies of the Japanese militarists, yet we are still neighbours to the Japanese people, who share with us a language of a common origin. Reviewing Japan's history and looking forward to her future, we not only see danger in her path but lament her lot.

Comrades, you should realize that the Japanese militarists are now heading blindly into a maze. They have forgotten their own history, their own position, and can neither see the outside world and their own crisis, nor recognize their neighbour, a revolutionary China. There are but two aspects to their thought. On the one hand they are so blind to facts as vainly to hope that China might accept their outrageous terms, and on the other hand they rely on their cunning to achieve some tour-de-force and to benefit by hoodwinking the world. Because they themselves are stupid, they believe the peoples of the world are to be befooled. Because they themselves are violent, they believe that force can dominate this world.

As borne out by the terms embodied in his statement, [Japanese prime minister] Konoye wants to close China's Open Door and break the Nine-Power Treaty [signed in 1922 in Washington, D.C., and guaranteeing China its territorial integrity and establishing an "open-door" policy on Chinese trade] by establishing a so-called "new order in East Asia," and to expel European and American influence from China by creating a so-called "unity of East Asia" and "economic bloc," and to revive the Twenty-one Demands [an ultimatum made in 1915 by Japan for the economic exploitation of China] presented to [Chinese president] Yuan Shih-kai by "stationing troops in China" and setting aside "Inner Mongolia as a Special Area." Summing up, Japan intends to force China to destroy by her own hand the principles of Open Door and Equal Opportunity, the League of Nations Covenant, the Nine-Power Treaty, the Sino-Soviet Non-Aggression Pact and other international treaties, by resorting to such terms as "creating a new order in East Asia." They wish to bind our hands, squeeze our arteries, yet they expect us to follow in their footsteps by breaking faith and despising loyalty to hasten the realization of their domination in East Asia, after which they might direct the world. Throughout five thousand years, China has always been guided by good faith and sincerity, in her statecraft. How can we be made to yield by threats and abandon our stand?

China as a state is founded on the principles not to oppress the undefended, nor fear the aggressive. More particularly, she is not willing to violate pacts or break faith and thus destroy the righteous principles governing the relations of mankind. I remember the meeting of [Japanese prime minister Giichi] Tanaka and our late Tsungli (Dr. Sun Yat-sen) in Shanghai in the third year of the Republic [1914] which coincided with the outbreak of the Great War in Europe. Tanaka proposed that East Asiatics should at that time denounce all ratified relations with foreign countries and erect a new order in East Asia. Dr. Sun queried: "Would it not involve the breaking of international treaties?" To which Tanaka answered: "Is not the denunciation of treaties and termination of unequal obligations advantageous to China?" "Unequal treaties should be terminated by straightforward and legitimate procedure," solemnly declared Dr. Sun, "and China is not prepared to become a party to the illegal denunciation of treaties even though advantageous to our country." Comrades, such is China's spirit. It is also the spirit of the Three People's Principles. We have relied on this spirit to resist invasion; we have depended on this spirit to resist all forms of domination, force and violence. We should be sustained by this spirit to restore order in East Asia and offer it as a contribution towards enduring world peace.

To conclude, this war on the part of Japan is violent banditry brought about by the total collapse of morals and sound principles in that country. Insofar as China is concerned, we have courageously taken upon our shoulders the world responsibility of fighting for justice and righteousness. Of late, the Japanese militarists have lost their senses, and prompted by sheer inertia, are rapidly going the way to exceed all bounds and damage the civilization and happiness of mankind. Nations of the world which are bound by treaty obligations should have acted to maintain the sanctity of treaties and apply punitive measures against the aggressor so that light might have been restored to the present scene of impenetrable darkness. But the nations hesitated and looked on. China, unmindful of any sacrifice, however, took upon herself the immense responsibility at the time when the fate of righteousness and justice was in the balance.

Our object in prosecuting this war of Resistance, is to complete the task of national revolution and secure for China independence, liberty and equality. Internationally, our object is to support righteousness and justice, restore the prestige of treaties, and re-establish peace and order. This is a war between good and evil, between right and wrong. It is a war between justice and force, and a war between an abider by the law and a breaker of it. It is also a war between righteousness and brute-force.

A Chinese proverb says: "Virtue never lacks company; it will ever find support." The force of world justice will rise, and men of goodwill ultimately co-operate in the interests of rectitude. On our part, we should hold fast to our stand and fix our eyes steadfastly on our goal, and be firm in our determination. Our firmness should increase with greater difficulties, and our courage should rise with prolonged Resistance. The entire nation should carry on with oneness of heart. The final victory will be ours. I urge my comrades, our army, and our people to redouble their efforts in order to attain success.

Hitler's Plans for Europe

Adolf Hitler

After assuming power in January 1933, Adolf Hitler defied the Treaty of Versailles—the agreement that ended World War I—by rebuilding his armed forces, remilitarizing the Rhineland region of Germany, and denouncing the reparations payments to the victorious Allies. There was much more to Hitler's program, however, than merely tearing up the Versailles treaty. In Hitler's eyes, Germany was owed vengeance for the humiliation it had suffered, and the country needed more "living room" for its burgeoning population. By August 1939 the German war machine was ready for full-scale war. Although the annexation of Austria and Czechoslovakia had been accepted by the Western powers reluctant to go to war, the invasion of Poland would not be. But the coming war, in Hitler's view, could not be avoided: It was the natural consequence of German superiority. The attack on Poland would pave the way for a new European order, in which Germany would impose its fascist regime throughout Europe at the point of a sword.

On August 22, 1939, Hitler assembled Germany's military brain trust at his mountain retreat, Obersalzberg, and delivered the following speech. On August 28 he formally abrogated the 1934 nonaggression treaty signed between Germany and Poland; three days later, Germany staged a phony attack against a German radio transmitter along the Polish border at the town of Gliwice. Claiming that Poland had attacked Germany, Hitler ordered his army to invade just before dawn on September 1, the date that traditionally marks the start of World War I.

Excerpted from Adolf Hitler's speech delivered at Obersalzberg, August 22, 1939.

[T he] decision to attack Poland was arrived at in spring. Originally there was fear that because of the political constellation we would have to strike at the same time against England, France, Russia and Poland. This risk too we should have had to take. [German field marshal Hermann] Goring had demonstrated to us that his Four-Year Plan is a failure and that we are at the end of our strength, if we do not achieve victory in a coming war.

Since the autumn of 1938 and since I have realised that Japan will not go with us unconditionally and that [Italian dictator Benito] Mussolini is endangered by that nitwit of a King and the treacherous scoundrel of a Crown Prince, I decided to go with [Russian leader Joseph] Stalin. After all there are only three great statesmen in the world, Stalin, I and Mussolini. Mussolini is the weakest, for he has been able to break the power neither of the crown nor of the [Roman Catholic] Church. Stalin and I are the only ones who visualise the future. So in a few weeks hence I shall stretch out my hand to Stalin at the common German-Russian frontier and with him undertake to re-distribute the world.

Our strength lies in our quickness and in our brutality; [Mongol leader] Genghis Khan has sent millions of women and children into death knowingly and with a light heart. History sees in him only the great founder of States. As to what the weak Western European civilisation asserts about me, that is of no account. I have given the command and I shall shoot everyone who utters one word of criticism, for the goal to be obtained in the war is not that of reaching certain lines but of physically demolishing the opponent. And so for the present only in the East I have put my death-head formations in place with the command relentlessly and without compassion to send into death many women and children of Polish origin and language. Only thus we can gain the living space that we need. Who after all is today speaking about the destruction of the Armenians?

Colonel-General [Walther] von Brauchitsch has promised me to bring the war against Poland to a close within a few weeks. Had he reported to me that he needs two years or even only one year, I should not have given the command to march and should have allied myself temporarily with England instead of Russia for we cannot conduct a long war. To be sure a new situation has arisen. I experienced those poor worms [French premier Édouard] Daladier and [British prime minister Neville] Chamberlain in Munich. They will be too cowardly to attack. They won't go beyond a blockade. Against that we have our autarchy and the Russian raw materials.

Poland will be depopulated and settled with Germans. My pact with the Poles was merely conceived of as a gaining of time. As for the rest, gentlemen, the fate of Russia will be exactly the same as I am now going through with in the case of Poland. After Stalin's death—he is a very sick man—we will break the Soviet Union. Then there will begin the dawn of the German rule of the earth.

Hitler desired vengeance and dominion for Germany and sought to establish his fascist regime throughout Europe.

The little States cannot scare me. After [President Kemal Atatürk's] death Turkey is governed by cretins and half idiots. [King] Carol of Roumania is through and through the corrupt slave of his sexual instincts. The King of Belgium and the Nordic kings are soft jumping jacks who are dependent upon the good digestions of their over-eating and tired peoples.

We shall have to take into the bargain the defection of Japan. I save Japan a full year's time. The Emperor is a counterpart to the last Czar—weak, cowardly, undecided. May he become a victim of the revolution. My going together with Japan never was popular. We shall continue to create disturbances in the Far East and in Arabia. Let us think as "gentlemen" and let us see in these peoples at best lacquered half maniacs who are anxious to experience the whip.

The opportunity is as favourable as never before. I have but one worry, namely that Chamberlain or some other such pig of a fellow will come at the last moment with proposals or with ratting. He will fly down the stairs, even if I shall personally have to trample on his belly in the eyes of the photographers.

No, it is too late for this. The attack upon and the destruction of Poland begins Saturday early. I shall let a few companies in Polish uniform attack in Upper Silesia or in the Protectorate. Whether the world believes it is quite indifferent. The world believes only in success.

For you, gentlemen, fame and honour are beginning as they have not since centuries. Be hard, be without mercy, act more quickly and brutally than the others. The citizens of Western Europe must tremble with horror. That is the most human way of conducting a war. For it scares the others off.

The new method of conducting war corresponds to the new drawing of the frontiers. A war extending from [the Polish cities of] Reval, Lublin, Kaschau to the mouth of the Danube. The rest will be given to the Russians. [Foreign Minister Joachim von] Ribbentrop has orders to make every offer and to accept every demand. In the West I reserve to myself the right to determine the strategically best line. Here one will be able to work with Protectorate regions, such as Holland, Belgium and French Lorraine.

And now, on to the enemy, in Warsaw we will celebrate our reunion.

Neutrality and the Outbreak of War

Franklin D. Roosevelt

During the summer of 1939 the United States was still recovering from the effects of the Great Depression, an economic disaster that had brought unemployment, poverty, and hunger to millions of citizens. The bloodshed and turmoil of World War I had left Americans reluctant to become involved in any further foreign wars. Isolationists insisted that Europe's problems were not America's and that the United States was unprepared to fight. American neutrality had long been a byword of politicians seeking and winning elective office.

The Nazi drive on Poland of September 1939 convinced President Franklin D. Roosevelt that he would have to confront and defeat the isolationist movement. Although he would keep the United States neutral for the time being, he realized that a confrontation with Nazi Germany and the Axis powers was inevitable. To prepare for this event, Roosevelt would have to rouse the Americans to the Allied side. On September 3, 1939, the president delivered the following address over the national radio network.

My fellow Americans and my friends: Tonight my single duty is to speak to the whole of America. Until four-thirty this morning I had hoped against hope that some miracle would prevent a devastating war in Europe and bring to an end the invasion of Poland by Germany.

Excerpted from Franklin D. Roosevelt's radio address, September 3, 1939.

For four long years a succession of actual wars and constant crises have shaken the entire world and have threatened
in each case to bring on the gigantic conflict which is today
unhappily a fact. It is right that I should recall to your minds
the consistent and at times successful efforts of your Government in these crises to throw the full weight of the United
States into the cause of peace.

In spite of spreading wars I think that we have every right
and every reason to maintain as a national policy the fundamental moralities, the teachings of religion [and] the continuation of efforts to restore peace—because some day, though
the time may be distant, we can be of even greater help to a
crippled humanity. It is right, too, to point out that the unfortunate events of these recent years have, without question,
been based on the use of force and the threat of force. And it
seems to me clear, even at the outbreak of this great war, that
the influence of America should be consistent in seeking for
humanity a final peace which will eliminate, as far as it is
possible to do so, the continued use of force between nations.

It is, of course, impossible to predict the future. I have my
constant stream of information from American representatives and other sources throughout the world. You, the
people of this country, are receiving news through your ra-
dios and your newspapers at every hour of the day. You are,
I believe, the most enlightened and the best informed people
in all the world at this moment. You are subjected to no cen-
sorship of news, and I want to add that your Government
has no information which it withholds or which it has any
thought of withholding from you. At the same time, as I told
my Press Conference on Friday, it is of the highest importance that the press and the radio use the utmost caution to
discriminate between actual verified fact on the one hand,
and mere rumor on the other.

I can add to that by saying that I hope the people of this
country will also discriminate most carefully between news
and rumor. Do not believe of necessity everything you hear
or read. Check up on it first. You must master at the outset
a simple but unalterable fact in modern foreign relations between nations. When peace has been broken anywhere, the
peace of all countries everywhere is in danger. It is easy for

you and for me to shrug our shoulders and to say that conflicts taking place thousands of miles from the continental United States, and, indeed, thousands of miles from the whole American Hemisphere, do not seriously affect the Americas—and that all the United States has to do is to ignore them and go about its own business. Passionately though we may desire detachment, we are forced to realize that every word that comes through the air, every ship that sails the sea, every battle that is fought does affect the American future.

Let no man or woman thoughtlessly or falsely talk of America sending its armies to European fields. At this moment there is being prepared a proclamation of American neutrality. This would have been done even if there had been no neutrality statute on the books, for this proclamation is in accordance with international law and in accordance with American policy. This will be followed by a Proclamation required by the existing Neutrality Act. And I trust that in the days to come our neutrality can be made a true neutrality.

It is of the utmost importance that the people of this country, with the best information in the world, think things through. The most dangerous enemies of American peace are those who, without well-rounded Information on the whole broad subject of the past, the present and the future, undertake to speak with assumed authority, to talk in terms of glittering generalities, to give to the nation assurances or prophecies which are of little present or future value.

I myself cannot and do not prophesy the course of events abroad—and the reason is that because I have of necessity such a complete picture of what is going on in every part of the world, that I do not dare to do so. And the other reason is that I think it is honest for me to be honest with the people of the United States. I cannot prophesy the immediate economic effect of this new war on our nation but I do say that no American has the moral right to profiteer at the expense either of his fellow citizens or of the men, the women and the children who are living and dying in the midst of war in Europe.

Some things we do know. Most of us in the United States believe in spiritual values. Most of us, regardless of what church we belong to, believe in the spirit of the New Testament—a great teaching which opposes itself to the use of force, of armed force, of marching armies and falling bombs. The overwhelming masses of our people seek peace—peace at home, and the kind of peace in other lands which will not jeopardize our peace at home. We have certain ideas and certain ideals of national safety and we must act to preserve that safety today and to preserve the safety of our children in future years. That safety is and will be bound up with the safety of the Western Hemisphere and of the seas adjacent thereto. We seek to keep war from our own firesides by keeping war from coming to the Americas. For that we have historic precedent that goes back to the days of the Administration of President George Washington.

It is serious enough and tragic enough to every American family in every state in the Union to live in a world that is torn by wars on other Continents. And those wars today affect every American home. It is our national duty to use every effort to keep those wars out of the Americas. And at this time let me make the simple plea that partisanship and selfishness be adjourned; and that national unity be the thought that underlies all others. This nation will remain a neutral nation, but I cannot ask that every American remain neutral in thought as well. Even a neutral has a right to take account of facts. Even a neutral cannot be asked to close his mind or close his conscience. I have said not once but many times that I have seen war and that I hate war. I say that again and again. I hope the United States will keep out of this war. I believe that it will. And I give you assurance and reassurance that every effort of your Government will be directed toward that end. As long as it remains within my power to prevent, there will be no blackout of peace in the United States.

GREAT
SPEECHES
IN
HISTORY

The War in
the West

The Soviet Invasion of Finland

A.K. Cajander

Imitating the conquests of Adolf Hitler and his Nazi armies in Poland, Soviet leader Joseph Stalin ordered an invasion of Finland during the fall of 1939. The attack was preceded by demands made at the negotiating table and border incidents that the Soviet Union claimed as intolerable provocations. Although Finland had been Russian territory for most of the nineteenth century, it had won its independence after the Russian Revolution of 1917. One of the most important motives for Stalin's winter war against Finland, however, was the seizure and use of Baltic Sea ports and airfields, which had been lost twenty years earlier and which would give the Soviet Union a strategic advantage in the European war.

Unfortunately for Stalin, the winter war did not go as quickly or as easily as expected. The Finns put up a stout defense of their territory, tying down thirty Soviet divisions through the winter along a long, rugged, and very cold frontier. The war lasted six hard months before the Finns finally had to sue for peace in March 1940. In the meantime, Soviet Russia was humiliated in the eyes of Hitler, who in turn made his own underestimation of Soviet resolve in his invasion of Stalin's territory during the summer of 1941.

One week after the first Soviet attack, Finnish prime minster A.K. Cajander made the following speech to his countrymen, detailing the causes of the war and calling for a national effort to repel the Soviet invaders.

Excerpted from A.K. Cajander's speech in Helsinki, November 23, 1939.

The people of Finland stand in front of an unexpected incident. The events followed in quick succession and the total sequence of events emerged as a total surprise for the majority of the Finnish people.

It is hardly a wrong conclusion if one, trying to interpret the present flow of events around the world, sees it as an expansionist tendency of the great powers, a constant and understandable phenomenon in the world history . . . whether you consider it justified or not.

The Tsarist state had in its final days a strong westward drive down to the shores of the Atlantic Ocean. The independent status of Finland was an obstacle to this goal and this was the motive to end the internal home rule, the autonomic status of Finland. The years of oppression in Finland derived from that. This policy was essentially different from the benevolent policy employed by the previous Emperors, especially Alexander I and II, who therefore enjoyed an undivided love of the Finnish people. This new policy embittered and strained the relationship between Finland and Russia to the extreme.

History seldom follows a straightforward course. The great war [World War I] crushed the intentions of the Tsarist regime. Onto its ruins the Union of Socialist Soviet Republics was born. It recognised nations' rights to self-determination and it has on all occasions assured its willingness to maintain friendly relations [with] her neighbors. Even the independence of Finland was recognised by her.

Thus the end of the world war also brought independence to Finland, but not without pains. The new situation was stabilised only after a bloody campaign. During this Germany gave Finland strong support which is not forgotten in Finland. Equally unforgettable is the support given by the Western Powers and America to stabilise the independent status of Finland. That was followed by twenty happy years of peace and construction, years only seldom shaded by dark shadows.

A little bit over two months ago the Soviet Union approached the Finnish Cabinet making certain propositions which were explained as aiming at improvement of the security of St. Petersburg or Leningrad and at strengthening of the friendly relationship between Finland and the Soviet Union.

These proposals were not completely unexpected. The forthcoming talks concerning required improvements of Leningrad's security were anticipated in private conversations with some members of the Finnish Cabinet a considerable time ago.

As we all well remember, there were negotiations between the Western Powers and the Soviet Union to accomplish a pact. The issue of Leningrad's security—concerning the so-called indirect aggression and other similar subjects—were discussed in such a manner which could have threatened the independence of Finland and the Baltic countries. The government of England, however, did not support these attempts. This is remembered here with sincere gratefulness. There was no outcome in the negotiations which also caused the specific issue concerning Finland to fall through.

The Nazi-Soviet Pact

A new decisive turn of events in Europe and even in the whole world took place when Germany and the Soviet Union concluded a non-aggression pact which in some respect even exceeded the regular scope of such agreements.

The pact came like a bolt from the blue. In Finland it, however, was not a complete surprise. As early as 1937 a remark was made by a prominent foreign authority about the possibility of the Soviet Union and Germany concluding a pact, perhaps in the near future. But the very timing of this non-aggression pact was, I guess, a complete surprise to all of us. In certain Finnish circles this new agreement was greeted with considerable hopes. Expectations [were] that this relaxation of tensions, previously a prevailing feature between the Soviet Union and Germany, [would have] a peaceful effect on tension in the Baltic Sea and the countries around it. This presumption, however, disappeared soon. In the Finnish domestic politics this pact had a significant effect on the policies of the political parties. It evaporated the assumption that the Soviet Union and Germany were ideologically incompatible and as a consequence of this all kinds of political speculations based on this contradiction were crushed. You can say that this pact thus strengthened the basis for a domestic concordance in Finland.

The non-aggression pact between Germany and the Soviet Union was immediately followed by a war between Germany and Poland from which again a new war between the Western Powers and Germany ensued. A universal conflagration was ignited.

The Oslo [Scandinavian] countries, Finland included, declared themselves to be absolutely neutral in this campaign between the great powers. Despite their neutrality, Finland and other Oslo countries suffer continuously and heavily from the economic consequences of the great war. Furthermore, especially Holland, Belgium and Finland but Switzerland, too, have been able to keep to their neutrality only by maintaining an extremely efficient guard for their defense.

In the opposite case their declaration of neutrality would scarcely have been respected.

The Fall of Poland

When Poland was near to collapse the Soviet Union marched its troops into eastern Poland and occupied it. Simultaneously the Soviet People's Commissar for Foreign Affairs made it known to the governments of Finland and the Baltic countries, as well as to other countries, that it will conduct a policy of neutrality towards them.

The defection of a Polish submarine to Tallinn (the capital of Estonia) was at first brought out as an excuse for proposals made by the Soviet Union to Estonia, which then finally resulted in allocating important military bases to the Soviet Union in Paldiski (Baltischport), Saaremaa (Ösel) and Hiiumaa (Dagö). In quick succession similar events followed in Latvia and Lithuania. These three vigorous Baltic countries with their own characteristic old cultures and a splendid future ahead were overnight turned into more or less dependencies of the Soviet Union.

Especially depressing to us, the Finns, is the fact that among these countries faced by this unfavorable fate is the State of Estonia, our dear fraternal nation. A follow-up was also the mass departure of Germans from the Baltics where they over a time period of 600 years had made history and

. . . carried [high] the national flag of the German stock.

It was to be expected, when thinking about the previous conduct by the Soviet Union, that she would make similar proposals also to the Finnish government. It should be stated, however, that the previously expressed reasons for Soviet intentions towards Finland had, at least in two counts, disappeared. The only great power which could have earlier been a potential threat to Leningrad—. . . presumably along the southern coast of the Gulf of Finland—namely Germany, has concluded a non-aggression pact with the Soviet Union, which means that there exists no threat against the Soviet Union and Leningrad from there—without considering the overall present importance of Leningrad to the Soviet Union. And the new Soviet naval and air bases in Liepaja (Libau), Ventpils (Windau), Hiiumaa, Saaremaa and Paldiski permit, as disclosed by the Soviets, the Soviet Union to rule the Baltic Sea and thus the Gulf of Finland and up to the Gulf's farthest recess in front of Leningrad.

Judging from the present facts, all arguments about threats to Leningrad from the Finnish territory are very difficult to understand.

A request for negotiations with the Soviet government was received on the 5th of October. For over a month friendly discussions were carried out between the Finnish and Soviet Cabinets concerning concrete political issues of certain territorial exchanges to improve the security of Leningrad.

The Cabinet of Finland, after discussing with representatives of parliamentary groups and after consulting the highest military command, yielded to Soviet demands in order to maintain good neighborly relations so far as it could, as a representative of an independent nation, to increase the security of a foreign metropolis but without sacrificing Finland's own national security.

However, the Soviets have made propositions which are very far away from those which can be considered as prerequisites in securing Leningrad. If they were accepted it would have offended Finland's neutrality and damaged her opportunities to self-defence: it would have meant severing the southern defence line of Finland at two of its most important points and handing over its first-class fortifications to a foreign power. Thus it [would have] resulted in a severe decrease in the security of Finland. Such proposals were unacceptable to the Finnish government.

Because of lack of common ground for the negotiations they have been interrupted for the moment. This is very deplorable because Finland sincerely will maintain good relations to all her neighbors and sincerely wants to strengthen these relationships when it does not endanger Finland's own vital interests.

Finland Will Not Submit

Our nation's conscience is clear. She knows that her cause is right and she knows that things are duly conducted. In making her points of view known Finland has not needed or received instructions from foreign countries. Finland has shown towards the Soviet Union friendliness and compliancy up to such limit which only can be crossed by weakening Finland's own national security.

Finland will not submit herself to a role of a vassal country. We will not yield to this by someone waging a . . . war [of nerves] or trying to exhaust us or doing the contrary, by offering temptations. Finland will peacefully, with open eyes and determined mind, observe the events in the west and in the east, and as a peaceloving country, which always appreciates good neighborly relations, is at any time ready to continue the negotiations on a basis which does not risk the vital interests of Finland or her national values. No further concessions can be [granted] especially now when Finland herself gains nothing from these territorial exchanges.

Finland is convinced that it is advantageous to the real interests of the Soviet Union that she has as a neighbor a nation whose loyalty it can trust in all circumstances.

The global situation continues as tense, and this [forces] Finland among many other neutral countries to keep a considerable amount of men in arms as protectors of neutrality and to also be otherwise prepared.

The time for the first enthusiastic unanimity is gradually over. Everyday activities start again to gain ground. It is necessary to restore the regular ways of living. It is of no use to be constantly prepared for something unexpected but, on the other hand, we should at any time be prepared to adjust our efforts if the situation demands that. The present situation may continue for a long time. We have to accustom ourselves to live and work in these altered conditions. Figuratively speaking, we must learn to plough carrying rifles on our backs.

Industrial production, which to some extent was interrupted in the beginning of this alert period, has to be restored as fully as possible in this changed situation taking, of course, into account the altered commercial demand and difficulties in obtaining necessary raw materials. Both the economical and other activities have to [make] full use of available opportunities in the new conditions. At the present the cabinet should restrict its interference in the economical life only [as much as necessary].

The return to everyday life should not imply that the spirits should [fail]. We have to maintain the same high enthusiasm which has become very well manifested when young men openheartedly now join the military service, or when hundreds of thousands of women help the reservists and their relatives, or when the defence bonds are subscribed with unexpected intensity, and in the warm-hearted donations given by private citizens and by a multitude of organizations to various apt purposes. Even in . . . everyday life . . . , what is the most essential to the enthusiasm—a devoted patriotic spirit—must stand strong. The patriotic unanimity should not be weakened. Along with this all that causes discontent, disappointment or mental depression should be avoided and removed.

The danger is all but over. In our continent on both sides of the Rhine and the North Sea an unprecedented rise of tension is witnessed. The time for its outbreak has not yet come but enormous forces are concentrated as a preparation for that. The exact time for the outbreak is not known but nobody can sincerely believe that this leads to nothing. And when the tension on its time once explodes, its remote effects can be felt far away.

There are certain elements in the society who try to sow the seeds of dissension among us, especially at the grass root level. Beware of these elements! Their real effects are so insignificant that no factual relevance can be attributed to them. But abroad their significance can be exaggerated and thus be used to harm our country.

We have to keep together—as a unified nation—like we did at the time of our first challenge, as unanimous as a democratic nation relying on its free will can ever be. The spirits born from our ordeals should and will stand the hardships, too. But even at that moment when an immediate danger is over we have to stay together. All in all we are a small nation and the stability of our international status depends decisively on our unanimity.

The world attention has focused on us without our own active influence. We have been met with a large scale sympathy of nations. This state of affairs obliges us. Let us make it known that we are worthy of the sympathy the world both in speeches and deeds has shown to us.

But first of all let us be worthy of the challenge set upon us.

Every Finnish citizen has his own guard post and everyone is expected to stay alert on his post without defying anyone but firmly defending the rights of the Finnish nation.

We are obliged to this because of our history, we are obliged to this because of our nation's future.

The Aim of Nazi Germany Is Slavery

Édouard Daladier

The head of the French government since 1938, Édouard Daladier had taken a backseat to British prime minister Neville Chamberlain during the Munich negotiations, which had surrendered Czechoslovakia to Nazi Germany. Although he had appeased Adolf Hitler at Munich, Daladier had no illusions about the true nature of the Nazi regime. In March 1939, after Hitler invaded and annexed all of Czechoslovakia, the French government had promised to protect Poland—the obvious target of the next German aggression—in case of another attack. This time, or so Daladier hoped, there would be no appeasement. After the attack on Poland in September 1939, France and Britain did finally declare war on Germany. But the victors of World War I had grown complacent while Germany rearmed during the 1930s. They could do little more than enforce a blockade of Germany, which did nothing to prevent the swift German victory in the east.

The military leaders of France realized that there was little chance of victory—and great risk of catastrophic failure—should they decide to attack across the Siegfried Line, Germany's fortified defense line in the west. France stood its ground, although some French and British leaders hoped once again that Hitler might be satisfied with the conquests he had already made. Daladier did not share their optimism, however, and on January 29, 1940, in the midst of what historians have called "the Phony War," he delivered the following radio address describing his opinion of Hitler's true goal.

Excerpted from Édouard Daladier's radio address, January 29, 1940.

At the end of five months of war one thing has become more and more clear. It is that Germany seeks to establish a domination over the world completely different from any known in history.

The domination at which the Nazis aim is not limited to the displacement of the balance of power and the imposition of supremacy of one nation. It seeks the systematic and total destruction of those conquered by Hitler, and it does not treat with the nations which he has subdued. He destroys them. He takes from them their whole political and economic existence and seeks even to deprive them of their history and their culture. He wishes to consider them only as vital space and a vacant territory over which he has every right.

The human beings who constitute these nations are for him only cattle. He orders their massacre or their migration. He compels them to make room for their conquerors. He does not even take the trouble to impose any war tribute on them. He just takes all their wealth, and, to prevent any revolt, he wipes out their leaders and scientifically seeks the physical and moral degradation of those whose independence he has taken away.

Under this domination, in thousands of towns and villages in Europe there are millions of human beings now living in misery which, some months ago, they could never have imagined. Austria, Bohemia, Slovakia and Poland are only lands of despair. Their whole peoples have been deprived of the means of moral and material happiness. Subdued by treachery or brutal violence, they have no other recourse than to work for their executioners who grant them scarcely enough to assure the most miserable existence.

There is being created a world of masters and slaves made in the image of Germany herself. For, while Germany is crushing beneath her tyranny the men of every race and language she is herself being crushed beneath her own servitude and her domination mania. The German worker and peasant are the slaves of their Nazi masters while the worker and peasant of Bohemia and Poland have become in turn slaves of these slaves. Before this first realization of a mad dream the whole world might well shudder.

Nazi propaganda is entirely founded on the exploitation

of the weaknesses of the human heart. It does not address it-self to the strong or the heroic. It tells the rich they are going to lose their money. It tells the worker this is a rich man's war. It tells the intellectual and the artist that all he cherished is being destroyed by war. It tells the lover of good things that soon he would have none of them. It says to the Christian be-liever: "How can you accept this massacre?" It tells the ad-venturer—"a man like you should profit by the misfortunes of your country."

It is those who speak this way who have destroyed or confiscated all the wealth they could lay their hands on, who have reduced their workers to slavery, who have ruined all intellectual liberty, who have imposed terrible privations on millions of men and women and who have made murder their law. What do contradictions matter to them if they can lower the resistance of those who wish to bar the path of their ambition to be masters of the world ?

For us there is more to do than merely win the war. We shall win it, but we must also win a victory far greater than that of arms. In this world of masters and slaves, which those madmen who rule at Berlin are seeking to forge, we must also save liberty and human dignity.

"Blood, Toil, Tears, and Sweat"

Winston Churchill

Britain and France declared war on Germany after Adolf
Hitler's invasion of Poland in September 1939. Neville
Chamberlain's policy of appeasement had failed, and the
attack on Poland finally forced the British government to
recognize that it would have to fight. Britons needed in-
spiration and a new sense of mission, and they had to be
prepared for hard sacrifices in the days ahead. For this,
the British government turned to Winston Churchill.

Churchill had long been renowned as an orator. First
elected to the House of Commons in 1900, he had campaigned in British colonial wars in Asia and Africa and
had served as first lord of the admiralty at the outbreak
of World War I. After Britain's failed Dardanelles campaign against the Ottoman Turkish army, Churchill was
relieved of his post but later won appointment as minister
of munitions and then secretary of state for war and air.

Throughout the 1930s Churchill had been tirelessly
warning the British against the threat posed by Hitler and
Nazi Germany. On May 10, 1940, after the downfall of
Chamberlain, Churchill was asked to form a new government. On May 13, while German armies were driving into
Belgium, Holland, and France, the new prime minister delivered the following speech in the House of Commons.

O n Friday evening last I received His Majesty's commission to form a new administration. It was the evident wish and will of Parliament and the nation

Excerpted from Winston Churchill's speech to the House of Commons, May 13, 1940.

that this should include all parties, both those who supported the late Government and also the parties of the Opposition. I have completed the most important part of this task. A War Cabinet has been formed of five Members, representing, with the Opposition Liberals, the unity of the nation. The three party leaders have agreed to serve, either in the War Cabinet or in high executive office. The three fighting services have been filled. It was necessary that this should be done in one single day, on account of the extreme urgency and rigor of events. A number of other key positions were filled yesterday, and I am submitting a further list to His Majesty tonight. I hope to complete the appointment of the principal Ministers during tomorrow. The appointment of the other Ministers usually takes a little longer, but I trust that, when Parliament meets again, this part of my task will be completed, and that the administration will be complete in all respects.

I considered it in the public interest to suggest that the House should be summoned to meet today. Mr. Speaker agreed, and took the necessary steps, in accordance with the powers conferred upon him by the Resolution of the House. At the end of the proceedings today, the adjournment of the House will be proposed until Tuesday, May 21, with, of course, provision for earlier meeting if need be. The business to be considered during that week will be notified to Members at the earliest opportunity. I now invite the House, by the Resolution which stands in my name, to record its approval of the steps taken and to declare its confidence in the new Government.

To form an administration of this scale and complexity is a serious undertaking in itself, but it must be remembered that we are in the preliminary stage of one of the greatest battles in history, that we are in action at many points in Norway and in Holland, that we have to be prepared in the Mediterranean, that the air battle is continuous and that many preparations have to be made here at home. In this crisis I hope I may be pardoned if I do not address the House at any length today. I hope that any of my friends and colleagues, or former colleagues, who are affected by the political reconstruction, will make all allowance for any lack of ceremony with which it has been necessary to act. I would say to the House, as I said to those who have joined this Government: "I have nothing to offer but blood, toil, tears and sweat."

We have before us an ordeal of the most grievous kind. We have before us many, many long months of struggle and of suffering. You ask what is our policy? I will say: It is to wage war, by sea, land and air, with all our might and with all the strength that God can give us: to wage war against a monstrous tyranny, never surpassed in the dark, lamentable catalogue of human crime. That is our policy. You ask, What is our aim? I can answer in one word: Victory—victory at all costs, victory in spite of all terror, victory, however long and hard the road may be; for without victory, there is no survival. Let that be realized; no survival for the British Empire; no survival for all that the British Empire has stood for, no survival for the urge and impulse of the ages, that mankind will move forward towards its goal. But I take up my task with buoyancy and hope. I feel sure that our cause will not be suffered to fail among men. At this time I feel entitled to claim the aid of all, and I say, "Come, then, let us go forward together with our united strength."

A Call for French Resistance

Charles de Gaulle

In 1940 General Charles de Gaulle served as undersecretary of the French Department of War. Although de Gaulle had argued that France must prepare for the mechanized war of the future, the French army remained stuck in the past, still largely an infantry force that fought with antiquated weapons and tactics. The French army swiftly fell before the German advance during the spring of 1940. The Maginot Line, a string of fortified bunkers and gun emplacements meant to protect France from a German invasion, was simply outflanked by German tanks, air bombardment, mobile infantry, and artillery. France fell in a few weeks.

The stunning collapse convinced many French leaders that their best course of action was simply to cooperate with the Germans. Marshal Philippe Pétain, a hero of the French victory in World War I, arranged for the surrender and was appointed head of a collaborationist government in the town of Vichy. De Gaulle, meanwhile, fled France for Great Britain, where he organized a resistance movement among his fellow exiles.

On June 18 and 19, 1940, de Gaulle gave the following radio address calling on the people of France to join a grand resistance movement to fight the Nazi occupation of their country. For these remarks, the Vichy government tried and convicted de Gaulle of treason; although he was an exile and was therefore absent during the trial, he was sentenced to be executed.

Excerpted from Charles de Gaulle's radio addresses, June 18 and 19, 1940.

[June 18, 1940] The leaders who, for many years past, have been at the head of the French armed forces have set up a government.

Alleging the defeat of our armies, this government has entered into negotiations with the enemy with a view to bringing about a cessation of hostilities. It is quite true that we were, and still are, overwhelmed by enemy mechanized forces, both on the ground and in the air. It was the tanks, the planes, and the tactics of the Germans, far more than the fact that we were outnumbered, that forced our armies to retreat. It was the German tanks, planes, and tactics that provided the element of surprise which brought our leaders to their present plight.

But has the last word been said? Must we abandon all hope? Is our defeat final and irremediable? To those questions I answer—No!

Speaking in full knowledge of the facts, I ask you to believe me when I say that the cause of France is not lost. The very factors that brought about our defeat may one day lead us to victory.

For, remember this, France does not stand alone. She is not isolated. Behind her is a vast empire, and she can make common cause with the British Empire, which commands the seas and is continuing the struggle. Like England, she can draw unreservedly on the immense industrial resources of the United States.

This war is not limited to our unfortunate country. The outcome of the struggle has not been decided by the Battle of France. This is a world war. Mistakes have been made, there have been delays and untold suffering, but the fact remains that there still exists in the world everything we need to crush our enemies someday. Today we are crushed by the sheer weight of mechanized force hurled against us, but we can still look to a future in which even greater mechanized force will bring us victory. The destiny of the world is at stake.

I, General de Gaulle, now in London, call on all French officers and men who are at present on British soil, or may be in the future, with or without their arms; I call on all engineers and skilled workmen from the armaments factories who are at present on British soil, or may be in the future, to get in touch with me.

Whatever happens, the flame of French resistance must not and shall not die.

Tomorrow I shall broadcast again from London.

[June 19, 1940]

Frenchmen must now be fully aware that all ordinary forms of authority have disappeared.

Faced by the bewilderment of my countrymen, by the disintegration of a government in thrall to the enemy, by the fact that the institutions of my country are, incapable, at the moment, of functioning, I, General de Gaulle, a French soldier and military leader, realize that I now speak for France.

In the name of France, I make the following solemn declaration:

It is the bounden duty of all Frenchmen who still bear arms to continue the struggle. For them to lay down their arms, to evacuate any position of military importance, or agree to hand over any part of French territory, however small, to enemy control, would be a crime against our country. For the moment I refer particularly to French North Africa—to the *integrity* of French North Africa.

The Italian armistice is nothing but a clumsy trap. In the Africa of Clauzel, Bugeaud, Lyautey, and Noguès, honor and duty strictly enjoin that the French should refuse to carry out the conditions imposed by the enemy.

The thought that the panic of Bordeaux could make itself felt across the sea is not to be borne.

Soldiers of France, wherever you may be, arise!

Germany Treacherously Attacks the Soviet Union

Joseph Stalin

Adolf Hitler and Soviet leader Joseph Stalin signed the Nazi-Soviet pact in August 1939, just before the German invasion of Poland. Hitler knew he could not afford a two-front war, and he intended to keep the Soviet Union neutral through this treaty. In exchange for its cooperation, the Soviet Union was to have the right to occupy and govern the Baltic states of Latvia, Lithuania, and Estonia as well as the eastern half of Poland.

The conquest of France and the Low Countries (Luxembourg, Belgium, and the Netherlands) in 1940 had allowed Hitler to draw troops from his western front, and relentless air and submarine attacks kept Great Britain off balance. As 1940 wore on, and as Germany tallied new victories in Europe, Hitler grew convinced that a confrontation with the Soviet Union must eventually come, pact or no pact. Soviet occupation of the Baltic states, although agreed to in the secret protocol, presented a strategic disadvantage to Germany, which in Hitler's view would always be threatened by its powerful eastern neighbor. In the spring of 1941 Hitler made the fateful decision to violate the pact and gathered his armies in the east. On June 22, 1941, Germany launched a full-scale invasion of the Soviet Union.

Excerpted from Joseph Stalin's speech to the Russian people, July 3, 1941.

Operation Barbarossa, as Hitler called the invasion, caught the Red Army and Stalin completely unprepared. A political purge of Red Army officers during the late 1930s had greatly weakened the military, and Stalin had come to believe that Hitler would never attack the Soviet Union because of its vast size and harsh climate. For several days after the invasion, Stalin remained in a state of shock, unable to pull himself together and organize defenses and strategy. Finally, on July 3—two weeks after Operation Barbarossa began—he gave the following speech to rouse Soviet citizens to resist.

Comrades! Citizens! Brothers and Sisters! Men of our Army and Navy!

I am addressing you, my friends!

The perfidious military attack on our fatherland, begun on June 22 by Hitler's Germany, is continuing.

In spite of heroic resistance of the Red Army, and although the enemy's finest divisions and finest air-force units have already been smashed and have met their doom on the field of battle, the enemy continues to push forward, hurling fresh forces into the attack.

Hitler's troops have succeeded in capturing Lithuania, a considerable part of Latvia, the western part of White Russia, and a part of the western Ukraine.

The Fascist air force is extending the range of operations of its bombers and is bombing Murmansk, Orsha, Mogilev, Smolensk, Kiev, Odessa, and Sevastopol.

A grave danger hangs over our country.

How could it have happened that our glorious Red Army surrendered a number of our cities and districts to the Fascist armies?

Is it really true that German Fascist troops are invincible, as is ceaselessly trumpeted by boastful Fascist propagandists? Of course not!

History shows that there are no invincible armies, and never have been. Napoleon's army was considered invincible, but it was beaten successively by Russian, English, and German armies. Kaiser Wilhelm's German army in the period of the first imperialist war was also considered invincible, but it was beaten several times by Russian and Anglo-French forces, and was finally smashed by Anglo-French forces.

The same must be said of Hitler's German Fascist army today. This army has not yet met with serious resistance on the Continent of Europe. Only on our territory has it met serious resistance, and if as a result of this resistance the finest divisions of Hitler's German Fascist army have been defeated by our Red Army, it means that this army, too, can be smashed and will be smashed as were the armies of Napoleon and Wilhelm.

As to part of our territory having nevertheless been seized by German Fascist troops, this is chiefly due to the fact that the war of Fascist Germany on the U.S.S.R. began under conditions favorable for German forces and unfavorable for Soviet forces.

The fact of the matter is that troops of Germany, as a country at war, were already fully mobilized, and 170 divisions hurled by Germany against the U.S.S.R. and brought up to the Soviet frontiers were in a state of complete readiness, only awaiting the signal to move into action, whereas Soviet troops had little time to effect mobilization and move up to the frontiers.

The Pact with Hitler

Of no little importance in this respect is the fact that Fascist Germany suddenly and treacherously violated the nonaggression pact she concluded in 1939 with the U.S.S.R., disregarding the fact that she would be regarded as an aggressor by the whole world. Naturally, our peace-loving country, not wishing to take the initiative of breaking the pact, could not resort to perfidy.

It may be asked: how could the Soviet government have consented to conclude a nonaggression pact with such treacherous fiends as Hitler and [Nazi foreign minister Joachim von] Ribbentrop? Was not this an error on the part of the Soviet government? Of course not!

Nonaggression pacts are pacts of peace between two

states. It was such a pact that Germany proposed to us in 1939. Could the Soviet government have declined such a proposal? I think that not a single peace-loving state could decline a peace treaty with a neighboring state, even though the latter was headed by such fiends and cannibals as Hitler and Ribbentrop.

But that, of course, only on one indispensable condition—namely, that this peace treaty does not infringe either directly or indirectly on the territorial integrity, independence, and honor of a peace-loving state.

As is well known, the nonaggression pact between Germany and the U.S.S.R. is precisely such a pact.

What did we gain by concluding a nonaggression pact with Germany? We secured for our country peace for a year and a half and the opportunity of preparing its forces to repulse Fascist Germany should she risk an attack on our country despite the pact.

This was a definite advantage for us and a disadvantage for Fascist Germany.

What has Fascist Germany gained and what has she lost by treacherously tearing up the pact and attacking the U.S.S.R.?

She gained a certain advantageous position for her troops for a short period, but she has lost politically by exposing herself in the eyes of the entire world as a bloodthirsty aggressor.

There can be no doubt that this short-lived military gain for Germany is only an episode, while the tremendous political gain of the U.S.S.R. is a serious and lasting factor that is bound to form the basis for development of decisive military successes of the Red Army in the war with Fascist Germany. . . .

Fighting the Nazi Invasion

In case of a forced retreat of Red Army units, all rolling stock must be evacuated; to the enemy must not be left a single engine, a single railway car, not a single pound of grain or a gallon of fuel.

Collective farmers must drive off all their cattle and turn over their grain to the safekeeping of state authorities for transportation to the rear. All valuable property including nonferrous metals, grain, and fuel which cannot be withdrawn must without fail be destroyed.

In areas occupied by the enemy, guerrilla units, mounted and foot, must be formed, diversionist groups must be organized to combat enemy troops, to foment guerrilla warfare everywhere, to blow up bridges, roads, damage telephone and telegraph lines, and to set fire to forests, stores, and transports.

Joseph Stalin

In occupied regions conditions must be made unbearable for the enemy and all his accomplices. They must be hounded and annihilated at every step and all their measures frustrated.

This war with Fascist Germany cannot be considered an ordinary war. It is not only a war between two armies, it is also a great war of the entire Soviet people against the German Fascist forces.

The aim of this national war in defense of our country against the Fascist oppressors is not only elimination of the danger hanging over our country, but also aid to all European peoples groaning under the yoke of German Fascism.

In this war of liberation we shall not be alone.

In this great war we shall have loyal allies in the peoples of Europe and America, including German people who are enslaved by Hitlerite despots.

Our war for the freedom of our country will merge with the struggle of the peoples of Europe and America for their independence, for democratic liberties. It will be a united front of peoples standing for freedom and against enslavement and threats of enslavement by Hitler's Fascist armies.

In this connection the historic utterance of British Prime Minister [Winston] Churchill regarding aid to the Soviet Union and the declaration of the U.S.A. government signifying readiness to render aid to our country, which can only evoke a feeling of gratitude in the hearts of the peoples of the Soviet Union, are fully comprehensible and symptomatic.

Comrades, our forces are numberless. The overweening enemy will soon learn this to his cost. Side by side with the Red Army and Navy thousands of workers, collective farmers, and intellectuals are rising to fight the enemy aggressor. The masses of our people will rise up in their millions. The working people of Moscow and Leningrad already have commenced to form vast popular levies in support of the Red Army.

Such popular levies must be raised in every city that is in danger of an enemy invasion; all working people must be roused to defend our freedom, our honor, our country—in our patriotic war against German Fascism.

In order to insure a rapid mobilization of all forces of the peoples of the U.S.S.R., and to repulse the enemy who treacherously attacked our country, a State Committee of Defense has been formed in whose hands the entire power of the state has been vested.

The State Committee of Defense has entered into its functions and calls upon all our people to rally around the party of Lenin-Stalin and around the Soviet government so as self-denyingly to support the Red Army and Navy, demolish the enemy, and secure victory.

All our forces for the support of our heroic Red Army and our glorious Red Navy.

All the forces of the people—for the demolition of the enemy!

Forward, to our victory!

Calling for a Holocaust

Heinrich Himmler

Heinrich Himmler was chief of the SS, or Schutzstaffel, the
elite Nazi police organization charged with purging the
Third Reich of its enemies. In Adolf Hitler's ideology, such
enemies included not only political opponents but also
Jews, whom he considered a decadent and inferior "race."
Hitler blamed the Jews for the Great Depression, for the
advent of communism in the Soviet Union, and for Germany's defeat in World War I. There was no major social
problem that Hitler did not lay at their feet and that, in
his opinion, could not be solved by their destruction.

At a conference held in the Berlin suburb of Wannsee
in January 1942, the SS was given the authority to carry
out a mass extermination of the Jews. Under Himmler's
direction, the SS built and managed dozens of concentration camps in and outside of Germany in which to hold
and murder Jews and all other enemies of the state. In the
following speech, given to a group of German officers at
Posen on October 4, 1943, Himmler describes the moral
justification for the murder and enslavement of races he
considered inferior to that of the Germans, and he exhorts his listeners to set aside their weaknesses and hu-
manitarian impulses to implement the Final Solution.

O ne basic principle must be the absolute rule for the SS
man: we must be honest, decent, loyal, and com-
radely to members of our own blood and to nobody
else. What happens to a Russian, to a Czech, does not inter-

Excerpted from Heinrich Himmler's speech delivered at Posen, October 4, 1943.

est me in the slightest. What the nations can offer in good blood of our type, we will take, if necessary by kidnapping their children and raising them with us. Whether nations live in prosperity or starve to death interests me only in so far as we need them as slaves for our culture; otherwise, it is of no interest to me. Whether 10,000 Russian females fall down from exhaustion while digging an anti-tank ditch interests me only in so far as the anti-tank ditch for Germany is finished.

We shall never be rough and heartless when it is not necessary, that is clear. We Germans, who are the only people in the world who have a decent attitude towards animals, will also assume a decent attitude towards these human animals.

But it is a crime against our own blood to worry about them and give them ideals, thus causing our sons and grandsons to have a more difficult time with them. When someone comes to me and says, "I cannot dig the anti-tank ditch with women and children, it is inhuman, for it will kill them," then I would have to say, "you are a murderer of your own blood because if the anti-tank ditch is not dug, German soldiers will die, and they are the sons of German mothers. They are our own blood.". . .

I also want to refer here very frankly to a very difficult matter. We can now very openly talk about this among ourselves, and yet we will never discuss this publicly. Just as we did not hesitate on June 30, 1934, to perform our duty as ordered and put comrades who had failed up against the wall and execute them [a bloody purge of SA officers and men took place on that date, as ordered by Adolf Hitler], we also never spoke about it, nor will we ever speak about it. Let us thank God that we had within us enough . . . fortitude never to discuss it among us, and we never talked about it. Every one of us was horrified, and yet every one clearly understood that we would do it next time, when the order is given and when it becomes necessary.

I am now referring to the evacuation of the Jews, to the extermination of the Jewish people. This is something that is easily said: "The Jewish people will be exterminated," says every Party member, "this is very obvious, it is in our program—elimination of the Jews, extermination, will do." And then they turn up, the brave 80 million Germans, and each one has his decent Jew. It is of course obvious that the others are pigs, but this particular one is a splendid Jew. But of all those who talk this way, none had observed it, none had endured it. Most of you here know what it means when 100 corpses lie next to each other, when 500 lie there or when 1,000 are lined up. To have endured this and at the same time to have remained a decent person—with exceptions due to human weaknesses—had made us tough. This is an honor roll in our history which has never been and never will be put in writing, because we know how difficult it would be for us if we had Jews as secret saboteurs, agitators and rabble rousers in every city, what with the bombings, with the burden and with the hardships of the war. If the Jews were still part of the German nation, we would most likely arrive now at the state we were at in 1916/17.

Fascism and the Future

Francisco Franco

Led by Generalissimo Francisco Franco, the fascists of
Spain had won power after defeating the Republicans,
who favored the establishment of a social democratic state
and who had taken power during the 1930s. Franco had
staged a coup d'etat against the Republican government,
and in the civil war that followed, German and Italian
fighters and bombers supporting Franco's armies played a
crucial role. Franco defeated the Republicans and came to
power allied with the fascist governments of Germany and
Italy. Like many others, Franco saw fascism as the wave
of the future and as the harbinger of a new world order.
Spain would follow its best opportunity and join closely
with its fascist allies; in this way, the nation would emerge
from the political and economic chaos of what Franco
called the liberal world into a more prosperous future.

Franco gave the following speech on December 8,
1942, to other leaders of his Falangist political party. Despite his alliance with Adolf Hitler, however, Franco
would prove to be a reluctant ally for the Germans. He
set down difficult conditions for his cooperation with the
Axis, and he did not go along with Hitler's plans for attacking the British through Gibraltar, a British possession
lying at the southern tip of Spain. Franco fully believed in
the future of fascism, but unlike Hitler and Benito Mussolini, he would survive the war and continue to rule a
fascist government until the 1970s.

Excerpted from Francisco Franco's speech to the Falangist Party, December 8, 1942.

I want my first words inaugurating the task of this third national council of the Falange to be clear regarding the statement of our political faith.

For three years of war and for three years of what we wrongly called peace we have had to struggle on in concerted endeavor. No one will be astonished if now, when this phase may be considered overcome, we throw off whatever and whoever would like to deflect us from marching toward fulfillment of our movement.

On this depends the destiny of Spain and the preservation of her eternal values, the suppression of which would imply slavery and chaos. On this path we must be intransigent in exacting sacrifices from all for the benefit of our national unity—a guarantee of Spain's future. The people might not be with Spain, but what is inadmissible is that any one should be against Spain. The foundations of our policy were laid in the beginnings of our movement, when our youth prepared itself for fight and engendered a spirit of our crusade that they derived from our soundest traditions of spiritual values and merged them with the social yearnings of our times.

We are living through historical moments that have so complicated a nature that, just as external events produce reaction in the internal life of a nation, so the internal life has had effects beyond its frontiers. For this reason our political attitude sought to correlate our actions in the international sphere with the supreme needs of our own country.

We are actors in a new era in which we can have no truck with the mentality of the past. Spain's way of thinking cannot go back to the nineteenth century, accursed by so many false conceptions. It is necessary for Spaniards to abandon the old liberal prejudices and take a survey of Europe in order to analyze contemporary history.

The Weakness of the Liberal World

We do not belong to a world of our own, as distinct from Europe, even though we have our own characteristics and spiritual reserves.

All contemporary events show us we are witnessing the

end of one era and the beginnings of another; that the liberal world is going down a victim to its own errors, and with it are disappearing commercial imperialism, financial capitalism and mass unemployment. The happiness promised by the French revolution became nothing but barter business, competition, low wages and mass insecurity.

Wealth did not go hand in hand with equitable distribution. The important part of humanity was prey to misery. Freedom is impossible as long as bondage and want exist. Cleverly exploited Marxist slogans caught on with the masses because they deceitfully promised a change in the justice of the pressing situation.

The liberal world, in giving adult suffrage, made them conscious of their own strength. Then the revolutionary process, accelerated by various crises, started. During the last war Russian demobilization led to a situation in which communism seized power and established a barbarian dictatorship of the proletariat. A similar phenomenon manifested itself in Italy after the war, but Mussolini's genius instilled all just and human elements interested in the Italian revolution into the Fascistis' aims.

Mussolini welded the two elements closely and united his own heart into the synthesis of the fascist revolution—a social urge and a national idea. Later, Germany found a new solution for the popular yearnings in national socialism, which unites the national and social idea for the second time in Europe with the special peculiarities of race thirsting for international justice. Those are not isolated movements, but rather aspects of one and the same general movement and mass rebellion throughout the world. On the face, a new useful consciousness emerged, which reacts against the hypocrisy and inefficiency of the old systems.

Youth marched conscious of its historic responsibility toward a goal sensed but not clearly defined. The goal then was defined by current events and by the leaders. These facts should explain to many people why so many Spaniards welcomed the republic with naive emotion. . . . The greater the hopes, the greater the disillusionment. Anger, indignation and revulsion grew against the vile outfit. . . .

When the Russian Comintern was about to make [Spain

the] prey of communism, it was a national movement that saved it and gave hopes for the revolution, its channel and direction. Collaboration-organized youth of Spain was a new facet of the general movement of European youth, which twenty-five years ago launched forth in open rebellion against the old, decayed and senile selfishness. Liberalism succumbed to its impetus. Empty slogans and vacillations were swept overboard and the task attacked in a revolutionary manner.

In our opinion, this maturing youthful enthusiasm still represents the strongest and most positive social factor. There not only was a fusion with our national and social ideals, but also with our Catholic soul, our country's raison d'etre, our history and our greatness. The Spanish solution was a union between national and social forces with supremacy of spiritual forces. On those true, unassailable principles our whole political work was based and will appear greater as time passes.

What the masses of the people in England think is not different from what the German masses think, nor do the dissatisfied people of Old Europe think differently from the disinherited in New America. Liberal propaganda may distort these facts and hide the truth for a time, but in the end truth will prevail.

The moment of disillusionment is not far distant. When the war ends and demobilization begins the moment will arrive to settle accounts and to fulfill promises.

Then, whatever projects there may exist now, the historic destiny of our era will be settled, either according to the barbarous formula of bolshevist totalitarianism, or according to the spiritual, patriotic formula Spain offers us, or according to any other formula of the fascist nations. Neither the feelings of the most numerous social classes, nor the exigencies of the post-war economy, nor the grave problems facing nations, will allow any other path.

The Path of Fascism

Those are mistaken who dream of the establishment of democratic liberal systems in Western Europe, bordering on Russian communism. Those err who speculate on liberal peace agreements or a bourgeois solution.

The world is marching on other roads. And the sentiments by which it is animated are so strong and just that, be it victory or defeat, they will overrun whatever may try to stop them.

The problem is not to permit that brute force of the torrent to destroy everything in its way, but rather to canalize and harness it, so that it becomes the fertilizing element of the new era. For this reason, because we know that ours is the truth, and because we have labored for it for six years, we look upon events with serenity.

In these days our generations are not merely faced with territorial and political problems, but also with supreme issues of the existence of our faith, our civilization and our culture, which are now at stake once more. This makes our presence in the international sphere so very important. . . .

Neither the highest cause of all, God, a cause never better served than under our regime, nor the interests of the country, never as well defended as in our days, nor the general welfare of our nation, embodied in our restored economy, reborn industries and flourishing fields, are safe from our enemies. What price, in the face of these truths, those remnants of the old minority groups that still clutch their old ideas?

Is it permissible to indulge in differences and divergencies when the fate of the country is at stake? What interests us is how to reach our aim. We cannot make any truce while we are on the way. We are ready then to install—if Spain's interests demand—the traditional system that reigned through our history, under the condition that everything appertaining to the realization and lasting character of our national revolution is safeguarded.

Certain people wished to be in our ranks in order to create among us a controlling body or a new minority group. That could not be permitted. The phase that begins now is that of unity and perfection in work, and of preparing ourselves for the great moment that the world offers us. We have called you together to carry our work to completion. It is heralded by continuous triumphs of our State, magnificent work of our youth organizations, silent productive labor of our feminine section, and pious endeavors of our social institutions. But our country demands more from us. The essential task lies before the new national council. It may well be that life will become more difficult. Our paths are strewn with thorns, but there can be no flagging in pursuit of our ideals.

It is not enough to set our goal. It must be pursued with constancy and sacrifice. Fortitude, as well as good-will, is needed. When we have all this, the triumph will be complete, because we shall feel strong and secure. We have the strength of our truth, backed by the reality of our power. We promise a hard life, but a Spanish life worthy of our country and its destiny.

We do not work for ephemeral ends, but for a resplendent tomorrow. Our army has in it the flower of youth. Divine assistance clearly has shown itself to us. With it, nothing and nobody shall vanquish us. If we fought hard on our crusade, we would fight even harder if the new danger of new war should threaten us. We know that with us is life, without us, death.

Patton Explains the War

George S. Patton

General George S. Patton had commanded the armored
divisions in North Africa during Operation Torch, the
first U.S. initiative in the European theater. After the
North Africa campaign, Patton had led the U.S. invasion
of Sicily. Skillful and audacious in his tactics, Patton also
angered many fellow officers with his brusque manner
and independent streak. Patton got himself in trouble for
his harsh treatment of an American soldier suffering from
a bad case of battle fatigue. Patton had strong opinions
of his own on battle fatigue, and administered his treatment of the condition by slapping the soldier. For this, he
was called to account and was relieved of his command.

Good military commanders were still in demand. By
the spring of 1944, the United States and Great Britain
were preparing for the cross-channel invasion of the continent. In this campaign, Patton was appointed commander
of the Third Army, a force that would feign an invasion
across the English Channel at its narrowest point, toward
the French port of Calais, in order to divert and confuse the
German commanders. On May 17, 1944, just before the invasion of Normandy, Patton expounded on his theories of
war and victory in the following speech to American troops
assembled at Enniskillen Manor Grounds in England.

Men, this stuff some sources sling around about America wanting to stay out of the war and not wanting
to fight is a lot of baloney! Americans love to fight,

Excerpted from George S. Patton's speech given at Enniskillen Manor Grounds,
May 17, 1944.

traditionally. All real Americans love the sting and clash of battle. America loves a winner. America will not tolerate a loser. Americans despise a coward; Americans play to win. That's why America has never lost and never will lose a war.

You are not all going to die. Only two percent of you, right here today, would be killed in a major battle.

Death must not be feared. Death, in time, comes to all of us. And every man is scared in his first action. If he says he's not, he's a goddamn liar. Some men are cowards, yes, but they fight just the same, or get the hell slammed out of them.

The real hero is the man who fights even though he's scared. Some get over their fright in a minute, under fire; others take an hour; for some it takes days; but a real man will never let the fear of death overpower his honor, his sense of duty, to his country and to his manhood.

All through your Army careers, you've been bitching about what you call "chicken-shit drills." That, like everything else in the Army, has a definite purpose. That purpose is instant obedience to orders and to create and maintain constant alertness! This must be bred into every soldier. A man must be alert all the time if he expects to stay alive. If not, some German son-of-a-bitch will sneak up behind him with a sock full of shit! There are four hundred neatly marked graves somewhere in Sicily, all because one man went to sleep on his job—but they are German graves, because we caught the bastards asleep!

An Army is a team, lives, sleeps, fights, and eats as a team. This individual hero stuff is a lot of horse shit! The bilious bastards who write that kind of stuff for the *Saturday Evening Post* don't know any more about real fighting under fire than they know about fucking! Every single man in the Army plays a vital role. Every man has his job to do and must do it. What if every truck driver decided that he didn't like the whine of a shell overhead, turned yellow and jumped headlong into a ditch? What if every man thought, "They won't miss me, just one in millions?" Where in Hell would we be now? Where would our country, our loved ones, our homes, even the world, be? No, thank God, Americans don't think like that. Every man does his job, serves the whole. Ordnance men supply and maintain the guns and vast machinery of this war, to keep us rolling. Quartermasters bring up clothes and food, for where we're going, there isn't a hell of a lot to steal. Every last man on K.P. [kitchen patrol] has a job to do, even the guy who boils the water to keep us from getting the G.I. shits!

Remember, men, you don't know I'm here. No mention of that is to be made in any letters. The USA is supposed to be wondering what the hell has happened to me. I'm not supposed to be commanding this Army, I'm not supposed even to be in England. Let the first bastards to find out be the goddamn Germans. I want them to look up and howl, "Ach, it's the goddamn Third Army and that son-of-a-bitch Patton again!"

We want to get this thing over and get the hell out of here, and get at those purple-pissin' Japs!!! The shortest road home is through Berlin and Tokyo! We'll win this war, but we'll win it only by showing the enemy we have more guts than they have or ever will have! There's one great thing you men can say when it's all over and you're home once more. You can thank God that twenty years from now, when you're sitting around the fireside with your grandson on your knee and he asks you what you did in the war, you won't have to shift him to the other knee, cough, and say, "I shoveled shit in Louisiana."

GREAT
SPEECHES
IN
HISTORY

The War
in Asia

The Attack on Pearl Harbor

Franklin D. Roosevelt

On the morning of December 7, 1941, a massive force of Japanese fighters, high-level and torpedo bombers, and submarines carried out a surprise attack on the U.S. naval and air station at Pearl Harbor, Hawaii. The attack achieved total surprise and resulted in heavy losses in ships, planes, and personnel. Coordinated with assaults on other bases in Guam, Wake Island, and the Philippines, the attack nearly achieved its objective of rendering the United States helpless to prevent further Japanese aggression in eastern Asia.

The end result of the attack on Pearl Harbor, however, was not what Japan had anticipated. The United States still had a powerful force of aircraft carriers in the Pacific, all of which had been safely out of harbor on the morning of December 7. Instead of disabling the U.S. military, the attack instantly roused the United States out of its neutrality in the war. Realizing that a long-expected opportunity had finally come, President Franklin D. Roosevelt delivered the following speech to a joint session of the U.S. Congress. Roosevelt describes in eloquent detail the attacks of the previous day and asks Congress for a declaration of war on Japan—a declaration that would come quickly and with only one dissenting vote.

Excerpted from Franklin D. Roosevelt's speech delivered to a joint session of Congress, December 8, 1941.

Yesterday, Dec. 7, 1941—a date which will live in infamy—the United States of America was suddenly and deliberately attacked by naval and air forces of the Empire of Japan.

The United States was at peace with that Nation and, at the solicitation of Japan, was still in conversation with the Government and its Emperor looking toward the maintenance of peace in the Pacific. Indeed, one hour after Japanese air squadrons had commenced bombing in Oahu, the Japanese Ambassador to the United States and his colleague delivered to the Secretary of State a formal reply to a recent American message. While this reply stated that it seemed useless to continue the existing diplomatic negotiations, it contained no threat or hint of war or armed attack.

It will be recorded that the distance of Hawaii from Japan makes it obvious that the attack was deliberately planned many days or even weeks ago. During the intervening time, the Japanese Government had deliberately sought to deceive the United States by false statements and expressions of hope for continued peace.

The attack yesterday on the Hawaiian Islands has caused severe damage to American naval and military forces. Very many American lives have been lost. In addition American ships have been reported torpedoed on the high seas between San Francisco and Honolulu.

Yesterday the Japanese Government also launched an attack against Malaya.

Last night Japanese forces attacked Hong Kong.

Last night Japanese forces attacked Guam.

Last night Japanese forces attacked the Philippine Islands.

Last night the Japanese attacked Wake Island.

Last night the Japanese attacked Midway Island.

Japan has, therefore, undertaken a surprise offensive extending throughout the Pacific area. The facts of yesterday speak for themselves. The people of the United States have already formed their opinions and well understand the implications to the very life and safety of our Nation.

As Commander-in-Chief of the Army and Navy I have directed that all measures be taken for our defense.

Always will we remember the character of the onslaught against us.

No matter how long it may take us to overcome this premeditated invasion, the American people in their righteous might will win through to absolute victory.

I believe I interpret the will of the Congress and of the people when I assert that we will not only defend ourselves to the uttermost but will make very certain that this form of treachery shall never endanger us again.

Hostilities exist. There is no blinking at the fact that our people, our territory, and our interests are in grave danger.

With confidence in our armed forces—with the unbounding determination of our people—we will gain the inevitable triumph—so help us God.

I ask that the Congress declare that since the unprovoked and dastardly attack by Japan on Sunday, December seventh, a state of war has existed between the United States and the Japanese Empire.

Japan's Destiny in Asia

Hideki Tojo

In the ten years since the Japanese invasion of
Manchuria, the Japanese army had conquered a large
swath of the Chinese mainland, driving the Chinese government from its capital and seizing cities, industries, and
ports. In 1937 the war in China spread from the capital
of Beijing and the port of Shanghai to the rest of the
country, and the Japanese under General Hideki Tojo had
conquered the Chinese coast as well as the valleys of the
Yellow and Yangtze Rivers. In 1938 Tojo joined the
Japanese cabinet as vice minister of war. He sought the
total rearmament of Japan to prepare for the coming
clash with the Allied powers and, eventually, with the Soviet Union over the occupation of Manchuria.

Under the government of Prince Fumimaro Konoe,
Tojo was appointed minister of war in July 1940. Tojo
led the faction within the Japanese government that was
for all-out war, with Great Britain as well as the United
States, in order to establish a permanent Japanese domination in what was called the Greater East Asia Prosperity Sphere. In this speech of May 27, 1942, Tojo describes Japan's victory and its glorious future to the
members of the Diet, or Japanese parliament.

O n this occasion of the opening ceremony of the Imperial Diet, I have no way to express my heartfelt
appreciation to have received the gracious Imperial

Excerpted from Hideki Tojo's speech given to the Japanese Diet, May 27, 1942.

Rescript [written pronouncement]. I have received the Sacred Message in reverence. . . .

I have sincere hopes above all [in] the fulfillment of the objective of the Sacred War. Ever since the outbreak of the Greater East Asia war, within a short period not yet exceeding the infant stage, our Imperial Forces have crushed the enemy forces wherever encountered and hence the most important bases . . . have been occupied one by one by our forces. American and British naval units have been annihilated in the Pacific Ocean and the Indian Ocean. In the face of these victories, this is the 8th Imperial Rescript conferred upon us. That our national prestige has been shown to the world has left a record unprecedented in the past. Moreover, accompanying the successive war victories unexampled in this world, new establishment is successfully being carried out in the various areas.

Here the objective of the Greater East Asia War is steadily being established. In concert with military operations in the southern regions, the activities of our Imperial Forces within the land are swiftly bringing about the destruction of Chungking's [China's] power. Furthermore, our defense in the northern direction has taken the form of a solid rock. The fighting power of the Imperial Forces is a gift of the August Virtue of the Emperor. I wish to express my deep gratitude to the men and officers of the Imperial Forces with the people of the nation, and I wish to pay my respects to the great number of the souls of valiant and courageous men. The various races in Greater East Asia that suffered greatly at the cruel treatment of America, Britain, and other countries in the past have been embraced within the spirit of one pillar supporting eight corners of the universe and have returned them to their original position. That they have been able to advance themselves a step toward the establishment of a new order is worthy of our mutual congratulation.

In concert with the great undertaking before us, the preparations for national defense have been strengthened and enlarged more than ever. However, the present situation which is advantageous for both within and without in the disposal of the war has opened the gates leading us to victory. It is needless for me to reiterate that the decisive battle for victory against America and Britain truly exists on the results of total war in the future. To the 100 million people of Japan that have received the Imperial Rescript of the Sacred War, I firmly believe that ever since the outbreak of the war the 100 million people are united under the Imperial message, their determination unchangeable and firm, and their faith immutable. The requirements and essence which guide the war in the future depend on the manifestations of the close cooperation extended by both army and navy in carrying out operations, expanding further the initial war results, as well as on the magnificent construction boldly carried out, thereby establishing measures to enhance the total war effort of the nation and strengthening a national structure of a sure victory. With unswerving faith and unchangeable determination, the Government expects to meet the faith of the people by fulfilling the heavy responsibilities of establishing the firm qualities in the foundation. . . .

The War Economy

At this time I should like to say a few words especially on the economic strength of Japan. In the first place, Japan's economy in the past had a strong tendency to rely on America and Britain. In regard to this the Government has extended deep consideration and has spent earnest effort to cover the weak aspects of Japan's economy. The government was strongly determined to establish a self-sufficient structure with respect to vital foodstuff and materials. As a result, the Government had made plans on the supply of vital materials which were necessary for national defense by establishing the 4-year plan. Consequently, immediately after the outbreak of the Greater East Asia war, Japan has taken means to oppose American and British oppression and has boldly established a strong economy that can decisively carry through the Greater East Asia war. The establishment of this economic power is truly the result of the extreme hardships undergone on the part of each and every Japanese subject, and in this respect I wish to express my innermost gratitude. The glorious war results achieved by the Imperial forces ever since the outbreak of the Greater East Asia war have taken management of the oil, tin, and rubber, and other supplying countries in the various areas in the southern regions; all these have fallen into our hands. As a result of mutual co-operation and self-sufficiency, which is the basis of Japan's economy, Japan's economy has become strong and firm more than ever. Hence, the materials of Japan, Manchoukuo [Manchuria] and China added with the materials of the various areas of the southern region, the foundation of Japan's self-sufficient production has been firmly established. Our wartime economy which occupies the front of our military power has reached its complete [heights] and has established a foundation of strengthening and expanding our military power. As for the future of [the] economy, it holds things very bright. However, in regard to enemy countries especially, which have relied on these various southern countries for materials vital to their national defense, the blows they are receiving are serious. . . .

In regard to Europe, the Imperial government at this time wishes to sincerely express its felicitation to Germany and Italy that are cooperating with Japan in the fulfillment of the same objective in this war and achieving great war results by overcoming various difficulties. America and Britain are undergoing a continuous change due to defeats suffered in this war and are carrying out vicious propaganda by constantly accusing our country of brutal acts. The fact that the countries of the world have been led by such a maneuver on the part of the distressed America and Britain has enabled them to realize that this has caused the grand union of the Axis countries that are extending political cooperation. The evil policies of America and Britain that have intended to live a life of ease and idleness on the many races and that have thought of their own progress only have been exposed to the world. At this time, as a result of sincerity shown by our imperial forces, the people of Burma in the various areas that are under the Japanese military administration of peaceful guidance have voluntarily brought upon themselves the chance to attain their independence. This is truly gratifying. The important defense bases of the [British] in India are falling into Japanese control. The golden opportunity for the people of India to win their independence has now come to the surface. The British-India negotiation led by [British diplomat Stafford] Cripps did not bear fruits. The fact that it had ended in utter failure makes us believe that India has given signs to depart from British rule and attain its independence spiritually. The spiritual foundation of Britain in India has become extinct. The first historical step of India's independence has truly started. However, today in India there still remains the skeleton structure of British domination and military facilities are still rooted, and the country itself is still subjected to oppression. As long as there remains British and American military facilities in India, Japan is strongly determined to completely destroy them.

As a result, it is truly unavoidable that the people of India are exposed to such a misfortune. At this time the people should be inspired with courage and destroy, wipe out the British and American forces. By completely wiping out British and American power, I greatly anticipate that the Indian people [will] realize their desire in the attainment of their independence. In connection with punitive operations carried out in Burma, Chungking government has been finally isolated and is at the threshold of destruction. In the first place as a result of earnest efforts of the Imperial forces, there are many who have surrendered and expressed their desire to cooperate with the [Japanese-dominated] Nanking Government. The power of the Chungking government is a thing of the past. Unless Chungking realizes its defeats . . . it shall continue to suffer as it has, and it is clear that the imperial forces are at the final stages [of crushing] the determination of the Chungking forces to offer resistance.

Japan's Victory in the Pacific

By the close and joint operation of Imperial army and naval forces the southwestern Pacific has completely fallen into our control. Australia has become the orphan of the Pacific Ocean. . . . In the Coral Sea battle carried out on the northern tip of Australia the American and British sea power has been crushed, and now there is no one before us to defend Australia. At this time I should like to emphasize again anew what I have said once before in the previous Diet meeting to the leaders of Australia, that they should survey the international situation, take into consideration Australia's geographical [jurisdiction], and decide upon their measures of disposal which at the present time is most important. At the present time, India is in confusion and in an unsettled state, Chungking is about to collapse, and Australia is isolated. As I review Shonan, Hongkong, and other important bases, peace and order being restored are steadily becoming the [foundation] of Greater East Asia establishment and are making great strides in its rebirth. Our sea power in the Pacific and the Indian Ocean is expanding day by day. Contrary to this, Britain has lost their overseas possessions and the route by which natural resources have been obtained has been taken control of by our forces. As a result it has added a great strain on the British domestic politics, and at the present time, Britain has reached a point of collapse. On the other hand, America that is suffering repeated defeats is trying to cover its mortal blow by relying on vicious propaganda and is in a desperate condition trying to cover the rising criticism within the country and to preserve the right of neutral countries.

To the people of America and Britain who are made victims of their leaders, I have no way to express my sympathy to them who are fighting for their leaders who value their commander with such character as to desert his comrades at the most crucial moment. . . . Moreover, Imperial Japan has firm confidence in the attainment of the ultimate victory in this sacred war and our military operations, which are magnificent and unparalleled in this world, are being boldly expanded. Hereafter, the Government has high hopes in the fulfillment of the Imperial wishes by attaining complete unity with the people, by managing the improvement and expansion of the total war effort of the nation, and by so doing tightening the strings of the helmet so that we may display ever more the ideal fighting spirit which is inherent of Imperial Japan and we may quickly bring about the fulfillment of our mission in the Holy War.

The bills which will be presented to the Diet concern measures for the firm operation of shipbuilding and others that are outstanding in the emergency situation. I earnestly desire that upon examination prompt approval be given on these bills. At the conclusion, in regard to the cooperation extended to Japan by the various axis nations, I wish to express my heartfelt appreciation, I also wish to express my deep respect to the greatest and united efforts of each and every Japanese subject.

The Alliance of China and India

Chiang Kai-shek

The bombing of Pearl Harbor brought the United States into the war at the side of Great Britain, whose colonies in eastern Asia also came under attack on the fateful day of December 7, 1941. Although the coordinated surprise attacks delivered a fearful blow to British assets in the region, it also clarified the situation for neutral countries and for the many European colonies of Asia: Japan was now striving for complete domination of southern and eastern Asia, and it would bring any nation it conquered into its Greater East Asia Prosperity Sphere, to forever serve as a source of raw materials and labor whenever needed by the Japanese military and Japanese industry.

Chiang Kai-shek, the leader of China's government, traveled to India in early 1942 to rally support for Great Britain among people and nations that had long been suffering under the British colonial occupation. Underlining the long history shared by the two great Asian civilizations, he made an appeal to the tradition of self-sacrifice also shared by the people of India and China. In his speech, he declared that the war would now force their two nations to look above self-interest and form a common front against the aggression of the Axis powers.

During my two weeks' stay in India I have had the opportunity of discussing very frankly with the highest civil and military authorities as well as with my In-

---

Excerpted from Chiang Kai-shek's speech to the people of India, February 21, 1942.

dian friends, questions concerning joint plans against aggression and the objective of our common efforts. I was happy to find that there was full sympathy and general understanding between us. . . .

China and India comprise one-half of the world's population. Their common frontier extends for nearly 2,000 miles. In the 2,000 years' history of their intercourse, which has been of a purely cultural and commercial character, there has never been an armed conflict. Indeed, nowhere else can one find so long a period of uninterrupted peace between two neighboring countries. This is an irrefutable proof that our two peoples are peace-loving by nature. Today they have not only identical interests but also the same destiny. For this they are in duty bound to side with the anti-aggression countries, and fight shoulder to shoulder to secure real peace for the whole world.

Moreover, our two peoples have an outstanding virtue in common—namely, the noble spirit of self-sacrifice for the sake of justice and righteousness; it is this traditional spirit which should move them to self-negation for the salvation of mankind. It is also this spirit which prompted China to be the first to take up arms against the aggressor countries, not merely for the purpose of securing her own freedom, but also for the purpose of securing justice and freedom for all mankind. I venture to suggest to my brethren, the Indian people, that in this most critical moment in the history of civilization, our two peoples should exert themselves to the utmost in the cause of freedom for all mankind, for only in a free world could the Chinese and Indian peoples obtain their freedom. Furthermore, should freedom be denied either to China or to India there could be no real peace in the world.

The present international situation divides the world into two camps, of aggression and anti-aggression. All those who opposed aggression and are striving for the freedom of their country and mankind should join the anti-aggression camp. There is no middle course, and there is no time to wait for developments. Now is the crucial moment for the whole future of mankind. The issue before us does not concern a dispute with any one man or country, nor does it concern any specific questions now pending between one people and another. Any people, therefore, which joins the anti-aggression front may be said to cooperate, not with any particular country, but with the entire front.

This leads us to believe that the Pacific war is a turning-point in the history of nationalism. The method, however, whereby the peoples of the world could attain their freedom might be different from what it used to be. The anti-aggression nations now expect that in this new era the people of India will voluntarily bear their full share of responsibility in the present struggle for the survival of that free world in which India must play her part.

The vast majority of the world's opinion is in full sympathy with India's aspirations for freedom. This sympathy, which is so valuable and so difficult to obtain, cannot be appraised in terms of money or material, and should therefore by all means be retained. The present struggle is one between freedom and slavery, between light and darkness, between good and evil, between resistance and aggression. Should the anti-aggression front lose the war, the civilization of the world would suffer a setback for at least 100 years, and there would be no end to human sufferings. . . .

In these horrible times of savagery and brute force, the people of China and their brethren the people of India should, for the sake of civilization and human freedom, give their united support to the principles embodied in the Atlantic Charter [a declaration of postwar aims agreed to by Prime Minister Winston Churchill and President Franklin Roosevelt in August 1941 in which the right of self-determination by sovereign nations was recognized] and in the joint declaration of the 26 nations, and ally themselves with the anti-aggression front. I hope the Indian people will wholeheartedly join the allies—namely, China, Great Britain, America and the Soviet Union—and participate shoulder to shoulder in the struggle for survival of a free world until complete victory has been achieved and the duties incumbent upon them in these troubled times have been fully discharged.

I sincerely hope, and I confidently believe, that our ally, Great Britain, without waiting for any demands on the part of the people of India, will as speedily as possible give them real political power, so that they may be in a position further to develop their spiritual and material strength and thus realize that their participation in the war is not merely an aid to the anti-aggression nations for the securing of victory, but also the turning-point in their struggle for India's freedom. From an objective point of view, I am of the opinion that this would be the wisest policy, which will redound to the credit of the British Empire.

Britain's Fight Is India's Fight

Mohandas Gandhi

The longtime occupation and exploitation of overseas colonies by Great Britain and the other European powers had convinced millions of people, including a majority in India, that the time had come to throw off the shackles of colonialism and achieve independence. The war in Europe seemed to afford an excellent opportunity to do just that. As France and Great Britain fought against Germany, pro-independence movements in Africa and Asia gained strength, some of them allying themselves directly with the Nazi government.

Mohandas Gandhi, the revered leader of India's drive for independence, had fought British colonialism for decades with speeches, articles, and nonviolent demonstrations. But at the outbreak of World War II, he concluded that India should ally itself with Britain in the fight against the Axis. Although the British government was promising self-determination for India after the war, imperial Japan was doing the opposite: attempting to make India a subservient nation. In the following speech to the All-India Congress, an assembly of representatives chosen solely by and for Indian communities, Gandhi declares his solidarity with Britain and his belief that British leaders could be counted on to keep their word and bring his long-sought goal: independence and true democracy in India.

Excerpted from Mohandas Gandhi's speech to the All-India Congress, August 7, 1942.

There are people who have hatred in their hearts for the British. I have heard of people saying that they are disgusted with them. The common people's mind does not differentiate between a Britisher and the imperialist form of their government. To them both are the same. There are people who do not mind the advent of the Japanese. To them, perhaps, it would mean a change of masters.

But it is a dangerous thing. You must remove it from your minds. This is a crucial hour. If we keep quiet and do not play our part, it will not be right.

If it is only Britain and the United States who fight this war, and if our part is only to give momentary help, whether given willingly or taken from us unwillingly, it is not a very happy proposition. But we can show our real grit and valor only when it becomes our own fight. Then every child will be brave. We shall get our freedom by fighting. It cannot fall from the skies.

I know full well that the British will have to give us our freedom when we have made sufficient sacrifices and proven our strength. We must remove the hatred for the British from our hearts. At least, in my heart there is no such hatred. As a matter of fact, I am a greater friend of the British now than I ever was.

The reason for this is that at this moment they are in distress. My friendship demands that I must make them aware of their mistakes. As I am not in the position in which they find themselves, I am able to point their mistakes out to them.

I know they are on the brink of the ditch, and are about to fall into it. Therefore, even if they want to cut off my hands, my friendship demands that I should try to pull them out of that ditch. This is my claim, at which many people may laugh, but all the same, I say this is true.

At the time when I am about to launch the biggest front in my life, there can be no hatred for the British in my heart. The thought that, because they are in difficulties, I should give them a push is totally absent from my mind. It has never been there. It may be that, in a moment of anger, they might do things that might provoke you. Nevertheless, you should not resort to violence; that would put non-violence to shame.

When such things happen, you may take it that you will

not find me alive, wherever I may be. Their blood will be on your head. If you do not understand this, it will be better if you reject this resolution. It will redound to your credit.

How can I blame you for the things you may not be able to grasp? There is one principle in a fight, which you must adopt. Never believe, as I have never believed, that the British are going to fail. I do not consider them to be a nation of cowards. I know that before they accept defeat every soul in Britain will be sacrificed.

They may be defeated and they may leave you just as they left the people of Burma, Malaya and other places, with the idea of recapturing lost ground when they can. That may be their military strategy. But supposing they leave us, what happens to us? In that case Japan will come here.

The coming in of Japan will mean the end of China and perhaps Russia, too. In these matters, Pandit Jawaharlal Nehru is my guru. I do not want to be the instrument of Russia's defeat, nor China's. If that happened I would hate myself.

You know that I like to go at a rapid speed. But it may be that I am not going as rapidly as you would want me to. Sardar Patel [presumably Sardar Vallabhbhai Patel, president of the All-India Congress parliamentary committee] is reported to have said that the campaign may be over in a week. I do not want to be in a hurry. If it ended in a week it would be a miracle, and if this happened it would mean the melting of the British heart.

It may be that wisdom will dawn on the British and they will understand that it would be wrong for them to put in jail the very people who want to fight for them. It may be that a change may come in Jinnah's mind, too. [Mohammed Ali Jinnah was the president of the All-India Moslem League.]

Non-violence is a matchless weapon, which can help every one. I know we have not done much by way of non-violence and therefore, if such changes come about, I will take it that it is the result of our labors during the last twenty-two years and that God has helped us to achieve it.

When I raised the slogan "Quit India" the people in India, who were then feeling despondent, felt that I had placed before them a new thing. If you want real freedom, you will have to come together, and such a coming together will create true democracy—the like of which has not so far been witnessed or attempted.

I have read a good deal about the French Revolution. [Historian Thomas] Carlyle's work I read while in jail. I have great admiration for the French people, and Jawaharlal has told me all about the Russian Revolution.

But I hold that though theirs was a fight for the people it was not a fight for real democracy, which I envisage. My democracy means that every one is his own master. I have read sufficient history, and I have not seen such an experiment on such a large scale for the establishment of democracy by non-violence. Once you understand these things you will forget the differences between the Hindus and Moslems.

The resolution that is placed before you says:

"We do not want to remain frogs in a well. We are aiming at world federation. It can only come through non-violence. Disarmament is possible only if you use the matchless weapon of non-violence."

There are people who may call me a visionary, but I am a real bania [shrewd businessman] and my business is to obtain swaraj [home rule].

If you do not accept this resolution I will not be sorry. On the contrary, I would dance with joy, because you would then relieve me of tremendous responsibility, which you are now going to place on me.

I want you to adopt non-violence as a matter of policy. With me it is a creed, but so far as you are concerned I want you to accept it as policy. As disciplined soldiers you must accept it in toto, and stick to it when you join the struggle.

People ask me whether I am the same man I was in 1920. The only difference is that I am much stronger in certain things now than in 1920.

CHAPTER
FOUR

The Defeat
of the Axis

Germany Must Fight On

Adolf Hitler

By the beginning of 1945, Germany found itself on the defensive, its armies in retreat. The western front was under attack by coordinated British, French, and American armies approaching the Rhine River. Its eastern front was crumbling before an onslaught by the immense Red Army of the Soviet Union. Germany's army, navy, and air force had been decimated after more than five years of war, and large swaths of its cities and ports lay in ruins from a constant pummeling by the air forces of the Allies.

For Adolf Hitler, however, surrender was not an option. On the contrary, he saw his country's desperate strategic situation as a test of its strength and its resolve. Still under the delusion that his army could successfully counterattack, he saw the troubles that Germany suffered in the years after World War I as identical to those it now faced. The revolution had come—the National Socialist revolution, with Hitler at its head as the undisputed master of Germany. In Hitler's eyes, the Nazi revolution had restored Germany's pride and its place at the center of the world stage. On January 30, 1945, he attempted to rally the nation with the following speech, delivered to mark the twelfth anniversary of the National Socialist regime.

Twelve years ago, when, as the leader of the strongest party, I was entrusted by the deceased Reich President, [Field Marshal Paul] von Hindenburg, with the office

Excerpted from Adolf Hitler's radio address, January 30, 1945.

of Chancellor, Germany found herself faced with the same situation internally as the one that today faces it externally. The forces of economic destruction and annihilation of the Versailles dictate led to a situation that had gradually become a permanent one—namely, the existence of almost 7,000,000 unemployed, 7,000,000 part-time workers, a destroyed farmers' class, a ruined industry and a commerce that had become correspondingly prostrate.

The German ports were nothing but ship cemeteries. The financial situation of the country threatened at any moment to lead to a collapse not only of the state but also of the provinces and of the communities. The decisive thing, however, was this: Behind this methodical destruction of Germany's economy, there stood the specter of Asiatic bolshevism. It was there then, just as much as it is there today.

In the years before our assumption of power the bourgeois world was incapable of opposing this development effectively on a small scale, just as it is incapable of doing so today on a large scale. Even after the collapse of 1918 this bourgeois world had failed to realize that an old world was vanishing and a new one being born and that there is no use in supporting and thus artificially maintaining what has been found to be decayed and rotten, but that something healthy must be substituted for it. A social structure that had become obsolete had cracked and every attempt to maintain it was bound to fail.

It was no different from today on a large scale, when the bourgeois states are doomed and when only clearly defined and ideologically consolidated national communities can survive the most difficult crisis Europe has seen in many centuries.

We were granted only six years of peace after January 30, 1933. During these six years tremendous feats were achieved, and even greater ones were planned, so many and such huge ones that they caused envy among our democratic, impotent neighbors.

But this was decisive: That we succeeded during these six years, with superhuman exertions, to restore the German nation militarily—that is, to imbue it with the spirit of resistance and self-assertion rather than to equip it with a material war potential.

The horrid fate that is now taking shape in the east and that exterminates hundreds of thousands in the villages and market places, in the country and in the cities will be warded off in the end and mastered by us, with the utmost exertion and despite all setbacks and hard trials.

The Fight Against Bolshevism

But if this is possible at all, it is only because a change has taken place in the German people since 1933. If Germany today were the Germany envisaged by the Versailles Treaty, Europe would long since have been swept away by the hurricane from Central Asia. It is hardly necessary to argue with those eternal blockheads who maintain that an unarmed Germany would, owing to its impotence, not have become the victim of this Jewish international world plot. Such reasoning would amount to a reversal of all laws of nature.

When was a helpless goose ever not eaten by the fox because she was constitutionally incapable of harboring aggressive designs? And when has a wolf ever reformed and become a pacifist because sheep do not wear armor? If there are still bourgeois states who earnestly believe this, that only proves how necessary it was to do away with an era that by its educational system managed to cultivate and maintain such notions, nay, even granted them political influence.

The fight against this Jewish Asiatic bolshevism had been raging long before National Socialism came into power. The only reason why it had not already overrun Europe during the years 1919–20 was that it was then itself too weak and too poorly armed.

Its attempt to eliminate Poland was not abandoned because of its compassion for the Poland of that time but only because of the lost battle before Warsaw. Its intention to annihilate Hungary was not discarded because they changed their minds, but because Bolshevist power could not be maintained militarily. Nor was the attempt to smash Germany given up because this achievement was not desired but because it proved impossible to overcome the natural resistance [and] stamina of our people.

Thereupon Judaism began systematically to undermine

our nation from within, and it found its best ally in those narrow-minded bourgeoisie who would not recognize that the era of a bourgeois world is ended and will never again return, that the epoch of unbridled economic liberalism has outlived itself and can only lead to its self-destruction and, above all, that the great tasks of our time can be mastered only under an authoritarian coordination of natural strength, based on the law of same rights for all and, thence, of same duties. On the other hand, the fulfillment of the same duties must necessarily entail an equality of rights.

Thus National Socialism, in the midst of gigantic economic, social and cultural reconstruction work, has also educationally given to the German people that armor without which no military values can be created.

The power of resistance of our nation has increased so tremendously since January 30, 1933, that it cannot be compared any more with that of former times. But the maintaining of this inner power of resistance is by the same token the safest guarantor of final victory. If Europe today finds itself stricken with a severe illness, the stricken countries will either overcome this illness by exerting their full and utmost power of resistance or they will succumb.

Yet the convalescent and survivor overcomes the climax of such an illness only in a crisis, a crisis that utterly weakens him, but in spite of all, it is all the more our immutable will not to shrink from anything in this battle for the salvation of our people from the most dreadful fate of all times and unflinchingly and faithfully to obey the law of the preservation of our nation.

God the Almighty has made our nation. By defending its existence we are defending His work. The fact that this defense is fraught with incalculable misery, suffering and hardships makes us even more attached to this nation. But it also gives us that hard will needed to fulfill our duty even in the most critical struggle; that is, not only to fulfill our duty toward the decent, noble Germans, but also our duty toward those few infamous ones who turn their backs on their people.

In this fateful battle there is therefore for us but one command: He who fights honorably can thus save his own life and the lives of his loved ones. But he who, because of cowardice or lack of character, turns his back on the nation shall inexorably die an ignominious death.

That National Socialism succeeded in awakening and strengthening this spirit in our German people is a great achievement. Only when this mighty world drama will have died away and the bells of peace are ringing will realization come of what the German people owes to this spiritual renaissance: No less than its existence in this world.

Germany and the Allies

Only a few months and weeks ago Allied statesmen openly outlined the German fate. Thereupon they were warned by some newspapers to be more intelligent and rather to promise something, even though nobody intended to keep this promise later.

As an inexorable National Socialist and a fighter for my people, I now wish to assure these statesmen once and for all that every attempt at influencing National Socialist Germany through slogans, lies and distortions presupposes a simple-mindedness unknown to the Germany of today. The fact that political activities and lies are inextricably linked in a democracy is of no consequence. Decisive is that every promise given by these statesmen to a people is today quite meaningless, because they are not in a position ever to fulfill any such promise. This is as if one sheep promised another sheep to protect it against a tiger.

I herewith repeat my prophecy: England will not only not be in a position to control bolshevism but her development will unavoidably evolve more and more toward the symptoms of this destructive disease.

The democracies are unable to rid themselves now of the forces they summoned from the steppes of Asia.

All the small European nations who capitulated, confident of Allied assurances, are facing complete annihilation. It is entirely uninteresting whether this fate will befall them a little earlier or later; what counts is its implacability. The Kremlin Jews are motivated only by tactical considerations; whether in one case they act with immediate brutality or, in another case, with some reticence, the result will always be the same.

Germany, however, shall never suffer this fate. The guarantor thereof is the victory achieved twelve years ago within our country. Whatever our enemies may plot, whatever sufferings they may inflict on our German cities, on German landscapes and, above all, on our people, all that cannot bear any comparison with the irreparable misery, the tragedy that would befall us if the plutocratic-Bolshevistic conspiracy were victorious.

Therefore, it is all the more necessary on this twelfth anniversary of the rise to power to strengthen the heart more than ever before and to steel ourselves in the holy determination to wield the sword, no matter where and under what circumstances, until final victory crowns our efforts.

On this day I do not want to leave any doubt about something else. Against an entire hostile world I once chose my road, according to my inner call, and strode it, as an unknown and nameless man, to final success; often they reported I was dead and always they wished I were, but in the end I remained victor in spite of all. My life today is with an equal exclusiveness determined by the duties incumbent on me.

Combined, they are but one: To work for my people and to fight for it. Only He can relieve me of this duty Who called me to it. It was in the hand of Providence to snuff me out by the bomb that exploded only one and a half meters from me on July 20, and thus to terminate my life's work. That the Almighty protected me on that day I consider a renewed affirmation of the task entrusted to me.

In the years to come I shall continue on this road, uncompromisingly safeguarding my people's interests, oblivious to all misery and danger, and filled with the holy conviction that God the Almighty will not abandon him who, during all his life, had no desire but to save his people from a fate it had never deserved, neither by virtue of its number nor by way of its importance.

Therefore I now appeal to the entire German people and, above all, to my old fellow-fighters and to all the soldiers to gird themselves with a yet greater, harder spirit of resistance, until we can again—as we did before—put on the graves of the dead of this enormous struggle a wreath inscribed with the words: "And yet you were victorious."

Therefore I expect every German to do his duty to the last and that he be willing to take upon himself every sacrifice he will be asked to make; I expect every able-bodied German to fight with the complete disregard for his personal safety; I expect the sick and the weak or those otherwise unavailable for military duty to work with their last strength; I expect city dwellers to forge the weapons for this struggle and I expect the farmer to supply the bread for the soldiers and workers of this struggle by imposing restrictions upon himself; I expect all women and girls to continue supporting this struggle with utmost fanaticism.

In this appeal I particularly address myself to German youth. In vowing ourselves to one another, we are entitled to stand before the Almighty and ask Him for His grace and His blessing. No people can do more than that everybody who can fight, fights, and that everybody who can work, works, and that they all sacrifice in common, filled with but one thought: to safeguard freedom and national honor and thus the future of life.

However grave the crisis may be at the moment, it will, despite everything, finally be mastered by our unalterable will, by our readiness for sacrifice and by our abilities. We shall overcome this calamity, too, and this fight, too, will not be won by central Asia but by Europe; and at its head will be the nation that has represented Europe against the East for 1,500 years and shall represent it for all times: our Greater German Reich, the German nation.

The Atomic Bomb Is Dropped on Japan

Harry S. Truman

By 1945 the war in the Pacific had become a fearsome war of attrition, with U.S. forces working their way from one island chain to the next in a series of desperately fought battles. The Japanese fought until death, using every weapon at their disposal, including a fleet of suicide bombers known as kamikazes, to stop the advance.

It was clear that the Japanese were losing the war. Still, like Germany, the Japanese refused to surrender, and the United States began to make plans for an invasion of Japan. Fearing the losses that would be suffered in such an invasion, President Harry S. Truman made the decision to use recently built and tested atomic weapons against Japanese cities. The presidential order went out on July 25. A squadron of bombers based on the island of Saipan was to proceed with the bombing at the first good weather opportunity after August 3. U.S. officials believed the incredible devastation and loss of life caused by these weapons would bring a swift Japanese capitulation.

On August 6 the first atomic bomb was dropped by the B-29 bomber *Enola Gay* on the city of Hiroshima. Three days later a second bomb was dropped on Nagasaki. More than one hundred thousand Japanese civilians lost their lives, and both cities were leveled. On the day of the second bombing, Truman made the following speech threatening even further destruction and demanding once again a final, unconditional Japanese surrender.

Excerpted from Harry S. Truman's speech on August 9, 1945.

The British, Chinese, and United States Governments have given the Japanese people adequate warning of what is in store for them. We have laid down the general terms on which they can surrender. Our warning went unheeded; our terms were rejected. Since then the Japanese have seen what our atomic bomb can do. They can foresee what it will do in the future.

The world will note that the first atomic bomb was dropped on Hiroshima, a military base. That was because we wished in this first attack to avoid, insofar as possible, the killing of civilians. But that attack is only a warning of things to come. If Japan does not surrender, bombs will have to be dropped on her war industries and, unfortunately, thousands of civilian lives will be lost. I urge Japanese civilians to leave industrial cities immediately, and save themselves from destruction.

I realize the tragic significance of the atomic bomb.

Its production and its use were not lightly undertaken by this Government. But we knew that our enemies were on the search for it. We know now how close they were to finding it. And we knew the disaster, which would come to this Nation, and to all peace-loving nations, to all civilization, if they had found it first.

That is why we felt compelled to undertake the long and uncertain and costly labor of discovery and production.

We won the race of discovery against the Germans. Having found the bomb we have used it. We have used it against those who attacked us without warning at Pearl Harbor, against those who have starved and beaten and executed American prisoners of war, against those who have abandoned all pretense of obeying international laws of warfare. We have used it in order to shorten the agony of war, in order to save the lives of thousands and thousands of young Americans.

We shall continue to use it until we completely destroy Japan's power to make war. Only a Japanese surrender will stop us.

The Surrender of Japan

Hirohito

Despite the atomic bombing of Hiroshima and Nagasaki, military advisers to Japan's Emperor Hirohito urged him to continue the fight. By this time, however, Japan's army was in retreat. The United States had established air bases on islands close to the Japanese archipelago and, with the Japanese air force decimated in the island campaign, was bombing Japan at will. If Japan remained defiant, there would be only one course left open to Japan's opponents: an invasion of the Japanese home islands. Hirohito also knew that the United States and the Soviet Union, which had just entered the war, were also making preparations to occupy and divide a defeated Japan—a humiliation that might endure for decades.

Hirohito made the final decision to surrender to the United States on August 14, 1945. On that day, the emperor made the following speech. His decision, however, was not accepted by a resolutely prowar faction within the military, which planned a coup d'etat against the emperor that was only stopped at the last minute by the emperor's supporters within the armed forces.

Hirohito's cooperation with the Allies at this point eventually convinced the United States to allow him to remain in power, a decision that would ease the acceptance by the Japanese of a future occupation by the United States.

Excerpted from Emperor Hirohito's speech to the Japanese people, August 14, 1945.

After pondering deeply the general trends of the world and the actual conditions obtaining in our empire today, we have decided to effect a settlement of the present situation by resorting to an extraordinary measure.

We have ordered our Government to communicate to the Governments of the United States, Great Britain, China and the Soviet Union that our empire accepts the provisions of their joint declaration.

To strive for the common prosperity and happiness of all nations as well as the security and well-being of our subjects is the solemn obligation which has been handed down by our imperial ancestors and which we lay close to the heart.

Indeed, we declared war on America and Britain out of our sincere desire to insure Japan's self-preservation and the stabilization of East Asia, it being far from our thought either to infringe upon the sovereignty of other nations or to embark upon territorial aggrandizement.

But now the war has lasted for nearly four years. Despite the best that has been done by everyone—the gallant fighting of the military and naval forces, the diligence and assiduity of our servants of the State and the devoted service of our 100,000,000 people—the war situation has developed not necessarily to Japan's advantage, while the general trends of the world have all turned against her interest.

Moreover, the enemy has begun to employ a new and most cruel bomb, the power of which to do damage is, indeed, incalculable, taking the toll of many innocent lives. Should we continue to fight, it would not only result in an ultimate collapse and obliteration of the Japanese nation, but also it would lead to the total extinction of human civilization.

Such being the case, how are we to save the millions of our subjects, or to atone ourselves before the hallowed spirits of our imperial ancestors? This is the reason why we have ordered the acceptance of the provisions of the joint declaration of the powers.

We cannot but express the deepest sense of regret to our allied nations of East Asia, who have consistently cooperated with the Empire toward the emancipation of East Asia.

The thought of those officers and men as well as others who have fallen in the fields of battle, those who died at their posts of duty, or those who met with death [otherwise] and all their bereaved families, pains our heart night and day.

The welfare of the wounded and the war sufferers and of those who have lost their home and livelihood is the object of our profound solicitude. The hardships and sufferings to which our nation is to be subjected hereafter will be certainly great.

We are keenly aware of the inmost feelings of all of you, our subjects. However, it is according to the dictates of time and fate that we have resolved to pave the way for a grand peace for all the generations to come by enduring the [unavoidable] and suffering what is unsufferable. Having been able to save and maintain the structure of the Imperial State, we are always with you, our good and loyal subjects, relying upon your sincerity and integrity.

Beware most strictly of any outbursts of emotion that may engender needless complications, of any fraternal contention and strife that may create confusion, lead you astray and cause you to lose the confidence of the world.

Let the entire nation continue as one family from generation to generation, ever firm in its faith of the imperishableness of its divine land, and mindful of its heavy burden of responsibilities, and the long road before it. Unite your total strength to be devoted to the construction for the future. Cultivate the ways of rectitude, nobility of spirit, and work with resolution so that you may enhance the innate glory of the Imperial State and keep pace with the progress of the world.

The Future of Japan

Naruhiko Higashikuni

Despite the steady advance of the American and British forces in Asia and the devastating atomic attacks on Hiroshima and Nagasaki, the decision to surrender was not universally accepted in Japan. The humiliation of the formal surrender ceremony in Tokyo Bay reminded many Japanese of their country's humiliation at the hands of the United States in 1854, when Commodore Matthew Perry threatened Japan with military action unless it opened its markets to Western trade. For many Japanese, total annihilation was preferable to a return to the country's former status as a subservient outpost of Western colonialism.

Realizing the strong opinions still in favor of war, and mindful of the pride and reverence the Japanese still felt for the emperor, Premier Naruhiko Higashikuni gave the following speech on September 5, 1945. The premier announces the acceptance of the surrender terms and describes the impossible economic and military situation that forced the surrender. He reminds his listeners of their duty to follow the command of the emperor, exhorts the Japanese to unite in the face of defeat, and promises cooperation with the United States in the rebuilding of the country.

U nder the recent Imperial proclamation Japan has accepted the joint declaration of America, Britain, China and the Soviet Union and through this extraordinary step the war of Greater East Asia has now been brought to an end. The termination of the war has been brought about solely through the benevolence of our sovereign. It was His Majesty himself who, in deference to the

---

Excerpted from Naruhiko Higashikuni's speech before the Japanese Diet, September 5, 1945.

spirits of the Imperial ancestors, decided to save millions of his subjects from privation and misery and to pave the way for an era of grand peace for generations to come.

Never before have we been moved so profoundly as by this act of boundless benevolence. With tears of overwhelming gratitude we can only offer our humble apologies for having troubled so much the august mind of our sovereign.

I am told that at the time immediately preceding the outbreak of war, when the Imperial Council was held to decide on the momentous question of peace or war, His Majesty was deeply distressed with the thought that should a world's major power like Japan cross swords with America and Britain it would bring on incalculable destruction and confusion that would be the worst imaginable calamity for humanity.

Expressing his desire to tide over the crisis and preserve the peace of the world by removing misunderstanding between Japan and the Anglo-Saxon countries, His Majesty exhorted the Council to do everything possible to reach an amicable settlement. All those in the Imperial presence were struck with awe at this manifestation of great and boundless benevolence.

The attitude of His Majesty in this regard underwent no change following the declaration of war and his mind, as deep and broad as the ocean, was always turned to the question of how to secure peace to the world.

Now owing to new developments in the situation Japan has had to terminate the war of Greater East Asia by an extraordinary step. This only serves to reveal the benevolent mind of His Majesty, set upon the cause of world peace.

The Causes of Defeat

As for the causes of our defeat, there are certainly more than one and they may well be left to historians of afterdays for unbiased study and criticism. There is little use of going back to the past, trying to put the blame upon one person or another.

We should rather reflect calmly upon our own conduct, each and every one of us, whether on the front or at home, whether in or out of the Government. A general repentance is demanded of the whole nation. We should purify . . . and start anew with fresh and chastened spirit, keeping in mind the lessons of the past.

Following the withdrawal of our forces from Guadalcanal, the war situation began to develop not always in our favor. Especially after the loss of the Marianas Islands, the advance of the Allied forces became progressively rapid, while the enemy's air raids on Japan proper were intensified, causing disastrous damages that mounted as the days went by.

The production of military supplies, which had been seriously affected by the curtailment of our marine transportation facilities, was dealt a severe blow by this turn of the war situation and almost insuperable difficulties began to multiply, beginning with spring of this year.

On the other hand, the general conditions of the country began to show marked signs of impoverishment and exhaustion with the continuation of the conflict, so much so that in the days just preceding the termination of the war it seemed almost impossible to carry on modern warfare further for any long period of time. . . .

Strangling the Japanese Economy

By May of this year our carrying capacity by steamboats had dwindled to about one-fourth of what we had at the beginning of the war, owing to the ever-increasing loss of ships and the diversion of bottoms [ships] to the South Seas area.

Moreover, the scarcity of liquid fuel and interference by the enemy caused a marked curtailment in the efficiency of shipping operations. Especially with the loss of the Okinawa Islands and the consequent increase in the striking power of the enemy's air forces, even communications with the China continent were rendered extremely hazardous.

The carrying capacity by motor and sailing vessels also was reduced rapidly and drastically through the insufficiency of fuel supply and interference by Allied forces. Such a general lowering in naval transportation capacity considerably affected the maintenance of our fighting power itself.

As regards railway transportation, frequent air raids together with depreciation of rolling stock and equipment brought about a steady lowering of its capacity and a tendency to lose unified control. On the whole, despite the exertion of all possible efforts, the carrying capacity of railways after the middle of the current year would have to be reduced, it was estimated, to less than one-half as compared with last year.

The excessive reduction of transportation capacity affected conspicuously [the use] of coal and other basic raw materials for industrial purposes and made well nigh impossible the importation of goods from the south. Moreover, various industries suffered directly from air raids which caused huge damages to plants and lowered the efficiency of the workmen. Finally, the country's production dwindled to such a point that any swift restoration of it came to be considered beyond hope.

Steel production was cut to less than one-fourth of the pre-war figure so that little could be expected regarding the construction of steel vessels. The conversion of materials on hand into fighting power also became more and more difficult of realization, owing to the dislocation of the system for coal distribution and the lack of minor transportation facilities.

As for coal, because of the wholesale reductions in land and sea transportation capacities, in addition to the steady decrease in output, the supply rapidly diminished, causing a general decline of industries in the vital zones of Japan, where even the closing of a large number of plants was expected.

As the importation of industrial salt from the continent diminished, the outputs of chemical industries based on the sodium industry had to decline with increasing rapidity and we were confronted since the middle of this year with a possibility that the supply of explosives and other indispensable materials as well as production of metals would be impeded.

The supply of liquid fuel already had been limited to what could be obtained in Japan, Manchuria and China. In the light of the shortage of oil stock and the difficulty of supplementing it, extraordinary efforts were devoted to an increase in the production of alcohol and pine root oil. However, the decrease of aircraft fuel was bound to cause serious effects in the near future upon the prosecution of the war.

In the meantime it was expected that the manufacture of modern war materials, principally aircraft, by mass production methods such as we had adopted before, would shortly have to face insurmountable difficulties as a result of the destruction of transportation and communications facilities caused by intensified air raids and shortages of fuel and materials. Thus our strength was rapidly weakened.

In May and June of this year, the basis of our material fighting resources to carry on modern warfare had been disastrously undermined. Even with all the measures adopted by the fighting services, the Government and the people in close cooperation, and their unparalleled endeavors for the restoration of national strength, it was feared that complete realization of our material resources would hardly be possible in the near future. The situation took a grave turn, particularly after the loss of Okinawa.

Moreover, the long period of war had caused increasing difficulties to the people's life, especially to the supply of foodstuffs, while the effects of inflation gradually were being felt by all classes of people, compelling careful consideration as regards the actual state of our fighting power.

The Decision to Surrender

In the meantime, the losses suffered by our forces in the many momentous battles during the protracted war had reached no small figures, although they succeeded in each battle to inflict heavy losses upon the Allied forces. Our losses in both naval and aerial strength were so enormous as to obstruct seriously the prosecution of the war.

But under the existing circumstances, as described above, the replenishment of these losses proved far from satisfactory. Our ground forces continued operations in various parts of Greater East Asia but it became hardly possible to provide them with adequate equipment. Our material fighting resources in the last days of the war thus were grievously deteriorating.

On the other hand, the capacity for supply and replenishment on the part of the Allied nations, with their vast resources and industrial power, was ever on the increase. Following up their victory over Germany, they collected their entire fighting strength around Japan, precipitating a break in the balance between our material fighting strength and theirs.

Such was the state of our national strength and the deterioration of the equipment of our armed forces. Regrettable as it was, the technical basis of our confidence in final victory was weakened and the war entered upon a really critical stage.

Meanwhile, air raids on Japan proper by Allied aircraft were steadily intensified. Medium and small cities, let alone great cities, were gradually destroyed in rapid succession with calamitous consequences. Two million, two hundred thousand houses were burned and hundreds of thousands of persons were killed and wounded, while the number of war sufferers approximates ten millions.

Moreover, in August the Allied forces started the use of the atomic bomb. The ruins of Hiroshima and Nagasaki, which were subjected to the attack of this bomb, are indeed too ghastly to look on. The terrific weapon was likely to result in the obliteration of the Japanese people and lead to the total extinction of human civilization.

Furthermore, the Soviet Union suddenly declared war on Japan, forcing us into the worst international situation. The United States, Britain and China previously had issued at Potsdam a joint declaration demanding the unconditional surrender of Japan. Under the existing circumstances Japan had to stand at the crossroads, whether to hope against hope in the desperate struggle involving the annihilation of her 100,000,000 people or to stop fighting.

The final and farsighted decision, however, was made by our sovereign, who is ever concerned about the future of the Japanese people and the peace of all mankind. It was decided to accept the terms of the Potsdam Declaration with the understanding that the declaration did not comprise any demand that would prejudice the prerogatives of His Majesty as the sovereign ruler.

The war of Greater East Asia has thus been brought to an end. The signature of the instrument of surrender took place between Japan and the Allied powers aboard a United States warship off Yokohama last Sunday. An Imperial proclamation was issued on the same day commanding all Japanese forces to cease hostilities and to lay down their arms.

With my heart full of deep emotion, I avail myself of this opportunity to express my profound gratitude to our allies in

Greater East Asia who spared no effort for the attainment of our common aims during the last four years of war.

Allied forces already are stationed in our country. This is really an unprecedented event and must be said to be the most serious situation our nation has ever faced in its history of 3,000 years.

It is the duty of us all to conform absolutely with the Imperial command and never depart from it. In obedience to the Imperial proclamation we should bear the unbearable and suffer what is unsufferable, admitting frankly the fact of our defeat of today, and fulfill manfully and faithfully with broadmindedness befitting a great nation the terms of the Potsdam Declaration and prove to all the world the true worth of our pledged word.

When I received the Imperial command to organize a new Cabinet, the Emperor was so gracious as to say to me: "Respect especially the Constitution and seek to solve the present problems by exerting your efforts toward control of the armed forces and the maintenance of law and order."

I was deeply moved, thinking of the anxieties shown by His Majesty regarding the present situation. Wishing only to obey His Majesty's word, I resolved to make it the fundamental principle of my administration, and I want to lead my fellow-countrymen by dedicating myself to the task of laying a foundation for a new and peaceful Japan, doing everything in my power. I wish that all the nation obey this . . . august command and march forward toward the realization of a new and prosperous era with fresh vigor and enthusiasm.

For that purpose it is most necessary, I believe, that there should spring up spontaneously a will toward reconstruction among our people through lively and free discussion and correct public opinion. Upon the formation of the present Cabinet I expressed my opinion to the effect that freedom of speech should be encouraged and freedom of organizing associations should be recognized.

Regarding freedom of speech and freedom of association, the Government intends to abolish temporary regulations governing publications, assemblies, associations, etc., at the earliest opportunity and already has mitigated the rules, as has been made public.

I am of the opinion that we should be very careful not to cool the ardor and zeal of the nation at all. It is my sincere wish that the Imperial Diet as an organ representing the nation will discharge its true function in accordance with the spirit of the Constitution so that it may reflect fairly the will of the people in fact as in name.

Rebuilding the Nation

Military and industrial demobilization is being carried out as a result of the termination of the war. People are to return to their homes and to their old occupations. The return to the homeland of large numbers of soldiers stationed in every quarter of Greater East Asia is indeed a tremendous task which will take, it is feared, a long time.

As regards the matter of affording help to these demobilized men, such as finding employment or promoting their welfare, the Government is leaving no stone unturned to make the necessary preparations, but it is desired that all people treat them with sympathy and fraternal feeling.

At this hour of national crisis, the turning point of our history, many difficulties will be encountered in our endeavors for post-war reconstruction in every direction. As stated in the rescript, the trials and tribulations that we have to undergo hereafter are not of an ordinary nature. Of course, the Government will do everything to insure the security of the nation's life involving problems of clothing, food and housing and intends to carry out necessary measures along all lines.

If there is anyone who dreams of going back quickly to the easy life of the pre-war days, he is wrong. With such an attitude, reconstruction for the future is unthinkable.

How to cope with the food situation of today is one of the most serious and difficult problems, since we cannot expect much by way of imports from Manchuria or other lands. It is a matter of course that the Government and people should cooperate in order to solve this problem.

As regards the problem of housing, an enormous number of houses was reduced to ashes during the war. Rebuilding is a matter of urgent necessity which permits of no delay. His Majesty, who is greatly concerned about the question, let it be known the other day that 1,000,000 koku [10,000,000 cubic feet] of timber would be granted as an Imperial gift to the people. The Government desires to solve housing problems as quickly as possible, taking measures such as construction of simple houses in large numbers.

The problem of clothing also is serious. Especially now when winter is not afar, the question of clothing, beds and . . . requires serious attention. In addition to the scarcity of textile products in stock and the difficulty of obtaining raw materials, the fact that most of the mills have been converted so as to meet military demands makes it very difficult for the moment to supply the nation with textile goods.

The Government will inaugurate various measures for restoring production facilities so as to supply as much clothing as possible, but at the same time it is desired that the difficulty on clothing will be mitigated more or less through voluntary donations of clothing by those who have not suffered from the war.

The blows dealt to the economy of our country by the war are very serious. . . . It cannot be denied that potential factors to create inflation are being fostered, one after another. When we consider the situation that is to arise in the wake of the post-war settlement, we must say that the burden on our economy will not lessen but will be made heavier by the termination of the war.

If the people should relax their determination or . . . fail to take any appropriate measures, inflation is bound to come, causing unmitigated destruction and confusion. The Government will do its best to prevent inflation and to take all possible measures to cope with the situation, but it is needless to say that efforts of the Government can bear fruit only with cooperation of all people.

To find employment for soldiers and workers who have been deprived of their jobs on account of demobilization and stoppages or reconversion of the munitions industry is an important problem as mentioned now in the disposal of post-war affairs. A considerable number of men are expected to be thrown out of work and the question of unemployment must be treated with special care as a problem of the administration, just as important as that of security of the nation.

For the time being the Government intends to divert such labor to agricultural production as much as possible.

New education, development of culture and reconstruction of industries all are big enterprises. And there are many more tasks to be undertaken. Only when those problems have been disposed of rightly and speedily will the foundation have been laid for construction along new lines.

The Government is resolved to move vigorously forward in order to solve all these problems, but much depends upon whether or not the people are equally determined in this regard and prepared to endure a hard life or privation. The road before us is long and beset with difficulties. But convinced of the imperishableness of our race and ever hopeful of the future of the Empire, let us toil unto the last.

"We are always with ye subjects." Such are the gracious words of our sovereign. Inspired thereby, let us resolve afresh to march forward in order to build a new Japan of peace and culture. Only in this manner shall we be able to set the august mind at ease and answer the spirits of the heroes who died in far and strange lands.

GREAT
SPEECHES
IN
HISTORY

The War's Legacy

The Iron Curtain

Winston Churchill

The war in Europe was over, but a new contest for power
had begun. This so-called Cold War pitted the Soviet
Union and its Communist allies against the United States
and its allies, notably Great Britain. Many historians
mark the Yalta Conference as the start of the Cold War.
The conference was attended by Winston Churchill,
Franklin D. Roosevelt, and Joseph Stalin in February
1945. In return for a promise to declare war on Japan
and aid the Allies in the Pacific theater of war, Stalin was
given control over the southern half of Sakhalin Island
and Manchuria and a free hand to extend Soviet government to the Baltic states, which the Red Army had occupied in 1939. Stalin also agreed to allow interim governments and free elections in the countries of Central
Europe liberated by the Soviet armies. These agreements
were never written down, however, and Stalin had no intention of keeping his promises.

Long a determined foe of communism, Winston
Churchill had set aside his hostility toward Soviet Russia
for the sake of a military alliance against Nazi Germany.
Once the war was over, Churchill began describing the
Cold War with the same dire warnings he had once delivered about the intentions of Adolf Hitler and Nazi Germany. In the following speech delivered at Westminster
College in Fulton, Missouri, on March 6, 1946, he coined
the phrase *Iron Curtain* to describe the imminent conquest of Central European nations by Soviet-allied governments and the division of Europe into two irreconcil-
able and well-armed camps.

Excerpted from Winston Churchill's speech delivered at Westminster College, Fulton, Missouri, March 6, 1946.

I am glad to come to Westminster College this afternoon, and am complimented that you should give me a degree. The name "Westminster" is somehow familiar to me. I seem to have heard of it before. Indeed, it was at Westminster that I received a very large part of my education in politics, dialectic, rhetoric, and one or two other things. In fact we have both been educated at the same, or similar, or, at any rate, kindred establishments.

It is also an honor, perhaps almost unique, for a private visitor to be introduced to an academic audience by the President of the United States. Amid his heavy burdens, duties, and responsibilities—unsought but not recoiled from—the President has traveled a thousand miles to dignify and magnify our meeting here to-day and to give me an opportunity of addressing this kindred nation, as well as my own countrymen across the ocean, and perhaps some other countries too. The President has told you that it is his wish, as I am sure it is yours, that I should have full liberty to give my true and faithful counsel in these anxious and baffling times. I shall certainly avail myself of this freedom, and feel the more right to do so because any private ambitions I may have cherished in my younger days have been satisfied beyond my wildest dreams. Let me, however, make it clear that I have no official mission or status of any kind, and that I speak only for myself. There is nothing here but what you see.

I can therefore allow my mind, with the experience of a lifetime, to play over the problems which beset us on the morrow of our absolute victory in arms, and to try to make sure with what strength I have that what has been gained with so much sacrifice and suffering shall be preserved for the future glory and safety of mankind.

The United States stands at this time at the pinnacle of world power. It is a solemn moment for the American Democracy. For with primacy in power is also joined an awe-inspiring accountability to the future. If you look around you, you must feel not only the sense of duty done but also you must feel anxiety lest you fall below the level of achievement. Opportunity is here now, clear and shining for both our countries. To reject it or ignore it or fritter it away will bring upon us all the long reproaches of the after-time. It is necessary that constancy of mind, persistency of purpose, and the grand simplicity of decision shall guide and rule the conduct of the English-speaking peoples in peace as they did in war. We must, and I believe we shall, prove ourselves equal to this severe requirement.

The Challenge of the Postwar World

When American military men approach some serious situation they are wont to write at the head of their directive the words "over-all strategic concept." There is wisdom in this, as it leads to clarity of thought. What then is the over-all strategic concept which we should inscribe today? It is nothing less than the safety and welfare, the freedom and progress, of all the homes and families of all the men and women in all the lands. And here I speak particularly of the myriad cottage or apartment homes where the wage-earner strives amid the accidents and difficulties of life to guard his wife and children from privation and bring the family up in the fear of the Lord, or upon ethical conceptions which often play their potent part.

To give security to these countless homes, they must be shielded from the two giant marauders, war and tyranny. We all know the frightful disturbances in which the ordinary family is plunged when the curse of war swoops down upon the bread-winner and those for whom he works and contrives. The awful ruin of Europe, with all its vanished glories, and of large parts of Asia glares us in the eyes. When the designs of wicked men or the aggressive urge of mighty States dissolve over large areas the frame of civilized society, humble folk are confronted with difficulties with which they cannot cope. For them all is distorted, all is broken, even ground to pulp.

When I stand here this quiet afternoon I shudder to visualize what is actually happening to millions now and what is going to happen in this period when famine stalks the earth. None can compute what has been called "the unestimated sum of human pain." Our supreme task and duty is to guard the homes of the common people from the horrors and miseries of another war. We are all agreed on that.

Our American military colleagues, after having proclaimed their "over-all strategic concept" and computed
available resources, always proceed to the next step—
namely, the method. Here again there is widespread agreement. A world organization has already been erected for the
prime purpose of preventing war, UNO [the United Nations
Organization], the successor of the League of Nations, with
the decisive addition of the United States and all that means,
is already at work. We must make sure that its work is fruitful, that it is a reality and not a sham, that it is a force for action, and not merely a frothing of words, that it is a true temple of peace in which the shields of many nations can some
day be hung up, and not merely a cockpit in a Tower of Ba-
bel. Before we cast away the solid assurances of national armaments for self-preservation we must be certain that our
temple is built, not upon shifting sands or quagmires, but
upon the rock. Anyone can see with his eyes open that our
path will be difficult and also long, but if we persevere together as we did in the two world wars—though not, alas, in
the interval between them—I cannot doubt that we shall
achieve our common purpose in the end.

I have, however, a definite and practical proposal to make
for action. Courts and magistrates may be set up but they cannot function without sheriffs and constables. The United Nations Organization must immediately begin to be equipped
with an international armed force. In such a matter we can
only go step by step, but we must begin now. I propose that
each of the Powers and States should be invited to delegate a
certain number of air squadrons to the service of the world
organization. These squadrons would be trained and prepared in their own countries, but would move around in ro-
tation from one country to another. They would wear the uniform of their own countries but with different badges. They
would not be required to act against their own nation, but in
other respects they would be directed by the world organization. This might be started on a modest scale and would grow
as confidence grew. I wished to see this done after the first
world war, and I devoutly trust it may be done forthwith.

It would nevertheless be wrong and imprudent to entrust
the secret knowledge or experience of the atomic bomb,

which the United States, Great Britain, and Canada now share, to the world organization, while it is still in its infancy. It would be criminal madness to cast it adrift in this still agitated and un-united world. No one in any country has slept less well in their beds because this knowledge and the method and the raw materials to apply it, are at present largely retained in American hands. I do not believe we should all have slept so soundly had the positions been reversed and if some Communist or neo-Fascist State monopolized for the time being these dread agencies. The fear of them alone might easily have been used to enforce totali-tarian systems upon the free dem-ocratic world, with consequences appalling to human imagination. God has willed that this shall not be and we have at least a breath-ing space to set our house in or-der before this peril has to be en-countered; and even then, if no effort is spared, we should still possess so formidable a superior-ity as to impose effective deter-rents upon its employment, or threat of employment, by others.

Winston Churchill

Ultimately, when the essential brotherhood of man is truly embodied and expressed in a world organization with all the necessary practical safeguards to make it effective, these powers would naturally be confided to that world organization.

Now I come to the second danger of these two marauders which threatens the cottage, the home, and the ordinary people—namely, tyranny. We cannot be blind to the fact that the liberties enjoyed by individual citizens throughout the British Empire are not valid in a considerable number of countries, some of which are very powerful. In these States control is enforced upon the common people by various kinds of all-embracing police governments. The power of the State is exercised without restraint, either by dictators or by compact oligarchies operating through a privileged party and a political police. It is not our duty at this time when difficulties are so numerous to interfere forcibly in the internal affairs of countries which we have not conquered in war. But we must never cease to proclaim in fearless tones the great principles of freedom and the rights of man which are the joint inheritance of the English-speaking world and which through Magna Carta, the Bill of Rights, the Habeas Corpus, trial by jury, and the English common law find their most famous expression in the American Declaration of Independence.

All this means that the people of any country have the right, and should have the power by constitutional action, by free unfettered elections, with secret ballot, to choose or change the character or form of government under which they dwell; that freedom of speech and thought should reign; that courts of justice, independent of the executive, unbiased by any party, should administer laws which have received the broad assent of large majorities or are consecrated by time and custom. Here are the title deeds of freedom which should lie in every cottage home. Here is the message of the British and American peoples to mankind. Let us preach what we practice—let us practice what we preach.

Friendship with the British

I have now stated the two great dangers which menace the homes of the people: war and tyranny. I have not yet spoken of poverty and privation which are in many cases the prevailing anxiety. But if the dangers of war and tyranny are removed, there is no doubt that science and co-operation can bring in the next few years to the world, certainly in the next few decades newly taught in the sharpening school of war, an expansion of material well-being beyond anything that has yet occurred in human experience. Now, at this sad and breathless moment, we are plunged in the hunger and distress which are the aftermath of our stupendous struggle; but this will pass and may pass quickly, and there is no reason except human folly or sub-human crime which should deny to all the nations the inauguration and enjoyment of an age of plenty. I have often used words which I learned fifty years ago from a great Irish-American orator, a friend of mine, Mr. Bourke Cockran. "There is enough for all. The earth is a generous mother; she will provide in plentiful abundance food for all her children if they will but cultivate her soil in justice and in peace." So far I feel that we are in full agreement. Now, while still pursuing the method of realizing our overall strategic concept, I come to the crux of what I have traveled here to say. Neither the sure prevention of war, nor the continuous rise of world organization will be gained without what I have called the fraternal association of the English-speaking peoples. This means a special relationship between the British Commonwealth and Empire and the United States. This is no time for generalities, and I will venture to be precise. Fraternal association requires not only the growing friendship and mutual understanding between our two vast but kindred systems of society, but the continuance of the intimate relationship between our military advisers, leading to common study of potential dangers, the similarity of weapons and manuals of instructions, and to the interchange of officers and cadets at technical colleges. It should carry with it the continuance of the present facilities for mutual security by the joint use of all Naval and Air Force bases in the possession of either country all over the world. This would perhaps double the mobility of the American Navy and Air Force. It would greatly expand that of the British Empire Forces and it might well lead, if and as the world calms down, to important financial savings. Already we use together a large number of islands; more may well be entrusted to our joint care in the near future.

The United States has already a Permanent Defense Agreement with the Dominion of Canada, which is so devotedly attached to the British Commonwealth and Empire. This Agreement is more effective than many of those which have often been made under formal alliances. This principle should be extended to all British Commonwealths with full reciprocity. Thus, whatever happens, and thus only, shall we be secure ourselves and able to work together for the high and simple causes that are dear to us and bode no ill to any. Eventually there may come—I feel eventually there will come—the principle of common citizenship, but that we may be content to leave to destiny, whose outstretched arm many of us can already clearly see.

There is however an important question we must ask

ourselves. Would a special relationship between the United States and the British Commonwealth be inconsistent with our over-riding loyalties to the World Organization? I reply that, on the contrary, it is probably the only means by which that organization will achieve its full stature and strength. There are already the special United States relations with Canada which I have just mentioned, and there are the special relations between the United States and the South American Republics. We British have our twenty years Treaty of Collaboration and Mutual Assistance with Soviet Russia. I agree with Mr. Bevin, the Foreign Secretary of Great Britain, that it might well be a fifty years Treaty so far as we are concerned. We aim at nothing but mutual assistance and collaboration. The British have an alliance with Portugal unbroken since 1384, and which produced fruitful results at critical moments in the late war. None of these clash with the general interest of a world agreement, or a world organization; on the contrary they help it. "In my father's house are many mansions." Special associations between members of the United Nations which have no aggressive point against any other country, which harbor no design incompatible with the Charter of the United Nations, far from being harmful, are beneficial and, as I believe, indispensable.

The Iron Curtain Falls

I spoke earlier of the Temple of Peace. Workmen from all countries must build that temple. If two of the workmen know each other particularly well and are old friends, if their families are inter-mingled, and if they have "faith in each other's purpose, hope in each other's future and charity towards each other's shortcomings"—to quote some good words I read here the other day—why cannot they work together at the common task as friends and partners? Why cannot they share their tools and thus increase each other's working powers? Indeed they must do so or else the temple may not be built, or, being built, it may collapse, and we shall all be proved again unteachable and have to go and try to learn again for a third time in a school of war, incomparably more rigorous than that from which we have just been released. The dark ages may return, the Stone Age may return on the gleaming wings of science, and what might now shower immeasurable material blessings upon mankind, may even bring about its total destruction. Beware, I say; time may be short. Do not let us take the course of allowing events to drift along until it is too late. If there is to be a fraternal association of the kind I have described, with all the extra strength and security which both our countries can derive from it, let us make sure that that great fact is known to the world, and that it plays its part in steadying and stabilizing the foundations of peace. There is the path of wisdom. Prevention is better than cure.

A shadow has fallen upon the scenes so lately lighted by the Allied victory. Nobody knows what Soviet Russia and its Communist international organization intends to do in the immediate future, or what are the limits, if any, to their expansive and proselytizing tendencies. I have a strong admiration and regard for the valiant Russian people and for my wartime comrade, Marshal Stalin. There is deep sympathy and goodwill in Britain—and I doubt not here also—towards the peoples of all the Russias and a resolve to persevere through many differences and rebuffs in establishing lasting friendships. We understand the Russian need to be secure on her western frontiers by the removal of all possibility of German aggression. We welcome Russia to her rightful place among the leading nations of the world. We welcome her flag upon the seas. Above all, we welcome constant, frequent and growing contacts between the Russian people and our own people on both sides of the Atlantic. It is my duty however, for I am sure you would wish me to state the facts as I see them to you, to place before you certain facts about the present position in Europe.

From Stettin in the Baltic to Trieste in the Adriatic, an iron curtain has descended across the Continent. Behind that line lie all the capitals of the ancient states of Central and Eastern Europe. Warsaw, Berlin, Prague, Vienna, Budapest, Belgrade, Bucharest and Sofia, all these famous cities and the populations around them lie in what I must call the Soviet sphere, and all are subject in one form or another, not only to Soviet influence but to a very high and, in many cases, increasing measure of control from Moscow. Athens alone—Greece with its immortal glories—is free to decide its future at an election under British, American and French observation. The Russian-dominated Polish Government has been encouraged to make enormous and wrongful inroads upon Germany, and mass expulsions of millions of Germans on a scale grievous and undreamed-of are now taking place. The Communist parties, which were very small in all these Eastern States of Europe, have been raised to pre-eminence and power far beyond their numbers and are seeking everywhere to obtain totalitarian control. Police governments are prevailing in nearly every case, and so far, except in Czechoslovakia, there is no true democracy. Turkey and Persia are both profoundly alarmed and disturbed at the claims which are being made upon them and at the pressure being exerted by the Moscow Government. An attempt is being made by the Russians in Berlin to build up a quasi-Communist party in their zone of Occupied Germany by showing special favors to groups of left-wing German leaders. At the end of the fighting last June, the American and British Armies withdrew westwards, in accordance with an earlier agreement, to a depth at some points of 150 miles upon a front of nearly four hundred miles, in order to allow our Russian allies to occupy this vast expanse of territory which the Western Democracies had conquered.

If now the Soviet Government tries, by separate action, to build up a pro-Communist Germany in their areas, this will cause new serious difficulties in the British and American zones, and will give the defeated Germans the power of putting themselves up to auction between the Soviets and the Western Democracies. Whatever conclusions may be drawn from these facts—and facts they are—this is certainly not the Liberated Europe we fought to build up. Nor is it one which contains the essentials of permanent peace.

The safety of the world requires a new unity in Europe, from which no nation should be permanently outcast. It is from the quarrels of the strong parent races in Europe that the world wars we have witnessed, or which occurred in former times, have sprung. Twice in our own lifetime we have seen the United States, against their wishes and their traditions, against arguments, the force of which it is impossible not to comprehend, drawn by irresistible forces, into these wars in time to secure the victory of the good cause, but only after frightful slaughter and devastation had occurred. Twice the United States has had to send several millions of its young men across the Atlantic to find the war; but now war can find any nation, wherever it may dwell between dusk and dawn. Surely we should work with conscious purpose for a grand pacification of Europe, within the structure of the United Nations and in accordance with its Charter. That I feel is an open cause of policy of very great importance.

In front of the iron curtain which lies across Europe are other causes for anxiety. In Italy the Communist Party is seriously hampered by having to support the Communist-trained Marshal [Josip] Tito's claims to former Italian territory at the head of the Adriatic. Nevertheless the future of Italy hangs in the balance. Again one cannot imagine a regenerated Europe without a strong France. All my public life I have worked for a strong France and I never lost faith in her destiny, even in the darkest hours. I will not lose faith now. However, in a great number of countries, far from the Russian frontiers and throughout the world, Communist fifth columns are established and work in complete unity and absolute obedience to the directions they receive from the Communist center. Except in the British Commonwealth and in the United States where Communism is in its infancy, the Communist parties or fifth columns constitute a growing challenge and peril to Christian civilization. These are somber facts for anyone to have to recite on the morrow of a victory gained by so much splendid comradeship in arms and in the cause of freedom and democracy; but we should be most unwise not to face them squarely while time remains.

The outlook is also anxious in the Far East and especially in Manchuria. The Agreement which was made at Yalta, to which I was a party, was extremely favorable to Soviet Russia, but it was made at a time when no one could say that the German war might not extend all through the summer and autumn of 1945 and when the Japanese war was expected to last for a further 18 months from the end of the German war. In this country you are all so well-informed about the Far East, and such devoted friends of China, that I do not need to expatiate on the situation there.

Looking at the Soviet Union

I have felt bound to portray the shadow which, alike in the west and in the east, falls upon the world. I was a high minister at the time of the Versailles Treaty and a close friend of Mr. [David] Lloyd-George, who was the head of the British delegation at Versailles. I did not myself agree with many things that were done, but I have a very strong impression in my mind of that situation, and I find it painful to contrast it with that which prevails now. In those days there were high hopes and unbounded confidence that the wars were over, and that the League of Nations would become all-powerful. I do not see or feel that same confidence or even the same hopes in the haggard world at the present time.

On the other hand I repulse the idea that a new war is inevitable; still more that it is imminent. It is because I am sure that our fortunes are still in our own hands and that we hold the power to save the future, that I feel the duty to speak out now that I have the occasion and the opportunity to do so. I do not believe that Soviet Russia desires war. What they desire is the fruits of war and the indefinite expansion of their power and doctrines. But what we have to consider here to-day while time remains, is the permanent prevention of war and the establishment of conditions of freedom and democracy as rapidly as possible in all countries. Our difficulties and dangers will not be removed by closing our eyes to them. They will not be removed by mere waiting to see what happens; nor will they be removed by a policy of appeasement. What is needed is a settlement, and the longer this is delayed, the more difficult it will be and the greater our dangers will become.

From what I have seen of our Russian friends and Allies during the war, I am convinced that there is nothing they admire so much as strength, and there is nothing for which they have less respect than for weakness, especially military weakness. For that reason the old doctrine of a balance of power is unsound. We cannot afford, if we can help it, to work on narrow margins, offering temptations to a trial of strength. If the Western Democracies stand together in strict adherence to the principles of the United Nations Charter, their influence for furthering those principles will be immense and no one is likely to molest them. If however they become divided or falter in their duty and if these all-important years are allowed to slip away then indeed catastrophe may overwhelm us all.

Last time I saw it all coming and cried aloud to my own fellow-countrymen and to the world, but no one paid any attention. Up till the year 1933 or even 1935, Germany might have been saved from the awful fate which has overtaken her and we might all have been spared the miseries Hitler let loose upon mankind. There never was a war in all history easier to prevent by timely action than the one which has just desolated such great areas of the globe. It could have been prevented in my belief without the firing of a single shot, and Germany might be powerful, prosperous and honored today; but no one would listen and one by one we were all sucked into the awful whirlpool. We surely must not let that happen again. This can only be achieved by reaching now, in 1946, a good understanding on all points with Russia under the general authority of the United Nations Organization and by the maintenance of that good understanding through many peaceful years, by the world instrument, supported by the whole strength of the English-speaking world and all its connections. There is the solution which I respectfully offer to you in this Address to which I have given the title "The Sinews of Peace."

Let no man underrate the abiding power of the British Empire and Commonwealth. Because you see the 46 millions in our island harassed about their food supply, of which they only grow one half, even in war-time, or because we have difficulty in restarting our industries and export trade after six years of passionate war effort, do not suppose that we shall not come through these dark years of privation as we have come through the glorious years of agony, or that half a century from now, you will not see 70 or 80 millions of Britons spread about the world and united in defense of our traditions, our way of life, and of the world causes which you and we espouse. If the population of the English-speaking Commonwealths be added to that of the United States with all that such co-operation implies in the air, on the sea, all over the globe and in science and in industry, and in moral force,

there will be no quivering, precarious balance of power to offer its temptation to ambition or adventure. On the contrary,
there will be an overwhelming assurance of security. If we ad-
here faithfully to the Charter of the United Nations and walk
forward in sedate and sober strength seeking no one's land or
treasure, seeking to lay no arbitrary control upon the
thoughts of men; if all British moral and material forces and
convictions are joined with your own in fraternal association, the high-roads of the future will be clear, not only for us
but for all, not only for our time, but for a century to come.

The Crimes of Nazi Germany

Robert H. Jackson

In the fall of 1945 twenty-two military and political leaders of Nazi Germany were arrested for war crimes and brought to the German city of Nuremberg. Over the next twelve months, an international military tribunal tried them in Nuremberg's Palace of Justice for conspiracy to wage aggressive war, waging aggressive war, war crimes, and crimes against humanity.

As the first criminal trial of civilian leaders by their victorious opponents, the Nuremberg trials caused controversy from the day the first indictments were handed down. The evidence and testimony, presented over months, did provide an exhaustive record of the deeds of Adolf Hitler and Nazi Germany and of the planning and carrying out of Germany's war in Europe. But many historians also point out that the selection of the defendants was arbitrary, and that no international law was binding on individuals. The trial satisfied those who demanded some form of accounting and punishment for Nazi Germany's crimes. But the dream of an international court of justice and international law that would prevent such misdeeds in the future has proved elusive.

Three of the accused at Nuremberg were acquitted, eight received prison sentences ranging from ten years to life in prison, and ten were executed. The twenty-second defendant, Hermann Göring, committed suicide before his sentence of death could be carried out. After Nuremberg, the hunt for Nazi criminals continued, with fugitives arrested, extradited, tried, and sentenced in Europe,

---

Excerpted from Robert H. Jackson's closing arguments at the Nuremberg war crimes trials, July 26, 1946.

South America, and Israel. Setting forth the justification
for these actions was Supreme Court justice Robert H.
Jackson, who delivered the following summation to the
Nuremberg trials on July 26, 1946.

M r. President and Members of the Tribunal: An advocate can be confronted with few more formidable tasks than to select his closing arguments
where there is great disparity between his appropriate time
and his available material. In 8 months [we] . . . have introduced evidence which embraces as vast and varied a
panorama of events as has ever been compressed within the
framework of a litigation. It is impossible in summation to
do more than outline with bold strokes the vitals of this
Trial's mad and melancholy record, which will live as the historical text of the twentieth century's shame and depravity.

It is common to think of our own time as standing at the
apex of civilization, from which the deficiencies of preceding
ages may patronizingly be viewed in the light of what is assumed to be "progress." The reality is that in the long per-
spective of history the present century will not hold an ad-
mirable position, unless its second half is to redeem its first.
These two-score years in the twentieth century will be
recorded in the book of years as one of the most bloody in
all annals. Two World Wars have left a legacy of dead which
number more than all the armies engaged in any way that
made ancient or medieval history. No half-century ever witnessed slaughter on such a scale, such cruelties and inhu-
manities, such wholesale deportations of peoples into slavery,
such annihilations of minorities. The terror of Torquemada
pales before the Nazi Inquisition. These deeds are the over-
shadowing historical facts by which generations to come will
remember this decade. If we cannot eliminate the causes and
prevent the repetition of these barbaric events, it is not an ir-
responsible prophecy to say that this twentieth century may
yet succeed in bringing the doom of civilization.

Goaded by these facts, we were moved to redress the
blight on the record of our era. The defendants complain that

our pace is too fast. In drawing the Charter of this Tribunal, we thought we were recording an accomplished advance in international law. But they say we have outrun our times, that we have anticipated an advance that should be, but has not yet been made. The Agreement of London, whether it originates or merely records, at all events marks a transition in international law which roughly corresponds to that in the evolution of local law when men ceased to punish crime by "hue and cry" and began to let reason and inquiry govern punishment. The society of nations has emerged from the primitive "hue and cry," the law of "catch and kill." It seeks to apply sanctions to enforce international law, but to guide their application by evidence, law, and reason instead of outcry. The defendants denounce the law under which their accounting is asked. Their dislike for the law which condemns them is not original. It has been remarked before that: "No thief e'er felt the halter draw with good opinion of the law.". . .

The Time for Final Judgment

But justice in this case has nothing to do with some of the arguments put forth by the defendants or their counsel. We have not previously and we need not now discuss the merits of all their obscure and tortuous philosophy. We are not trying them for the possession of obnoxious ideas. It is their right, if they choose, to renounce the Hebraic heritage in the civilization of which Germany was once a part. Nor is it our affair that they repudiated the Hellenic influence as well. The intellectual bankruptcy and moral perversion of the Nazi regime might have been no concern of international law had it not been utilized to goosestep the Herrenvolk across international frontiers. It is not their thoughts, it is their overt acts which we charge to be crimes. Their creed and teachings are important only as evidence of motive, purpose, knowledge, and intent.

We charge unlawful aggression but we are not trying the motives, hopes, or frustrations which may have led Germany to resort to aggressive war as an instrument of policy. The law, unlike politics, does not concern itself with the good or evil in the status quo, nor with the merits of the grievances against it. It merely requires that the status quo be not attacked by violent means and that policies be not advanced by war. We may admit that overlapping ethnological and cultural groups, economic barriers, and conflicting national ambitions created in the 1930's, as they will continue to create, grave problems for Germany as well as for the other peoples of Europe. We may admit too that the world had failed to provide political or legal remedies which would be honorable and acceptable alternatives to war. We do not underwrite either the ethics or the wisdom of any country, including my own, in the face of these problems. But we do say that it is now, as it was for sometime prior to 1939, illegal and criminal for Germany or any other nation to redress grievances or seek expansion by resort to aggressive war.

Let me emphasize one cardinal point. The United States has no interest which would be advanced by the conviction of any defendant if we have not proved him guilty on at least one of the Counts charged against him in the Indictment. Any result that the calm and critical judgment of posterity would pronounce unjust would not be a victory for any of the countries associated in this Prosecution. But in summation we now have before us the tested evidences of criminality and have heard the flimsy excuses and paltry evasions of the defendants. The suspended judgment with which we opened this case is no longer appropriate. The time has come for final judgment and if the case I present seems hard and uncompromising, it is because the evidence makes it so.

The Chief Villain

I perhaps can do no better service than to try to lift this case out of the morass of detail with which the record is full and put before you only the bold outlines of a case that is impressive in its simplicity. True, its thousands of documents and more thousands of pages of testimony deal with an epoch and cover a continent, and touch almost every branch of human endeavor. They illuminate specialities, such as diplomacy, naval development and warfare, land warfare, the genesis of air warfare, the politics of the Nazi rise to power, the finance and economics of totalitarian war, sociology, penology, mass psychology, and mass pathology. I must leave it to experts to comb the evidence and write volumes on their specialities, while I picture in broad strokes the offenses whose acceptance as lawful could threaten the continuity of civilization. I must, as [English writer Rudyard] Kipling put it, "splash at a 10-league canvas with brushes of comet's hair.". . .

The chief villain on whom blame is placed . . . is Hitler. He is the man at whom nearly every defendant has pointed an accusing finger.

I shall not dissent from this consensus, nor do I deny that

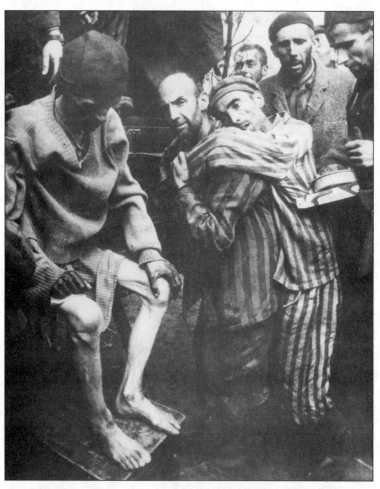

Concentration camp survivors endured demoralizing and horrific living conditions at the hands of the Nazis.

all these dead and missing men shared the guilt. In crimes so reprehensible that degrees of guilt have lost their significance they may have played the most evil parts. But their guilt cannot exculpate the defendants. Hitler did not carry all responsibility to the grave with him. All the guilt is not wrapped in [Heinrich] Himmler's shroud. It was these dead men whom these living chose to be their partners in this great conspiratorial brotherhood, and the crimes that they did together they must pay for one by one.

It may well be said that Hitler's final crime was against the land he had ruled. He was a mad messiah who started the war without cause and prolonged it without reason. If he could not rule he cared not what happened to Germany. As [Propaganda Minister Hans] Fritzsche has told us from the stand, Hitler tried to use the defeat of Germany for the self-destruction of the German people. He continued to fight when he knew it could not be won, and continuance meant only ruin. [Minister of Armaments Albert] Speer, in this courtroom, has described it as follows:

> The sacrifices which were made on both sides after January 1945 were without sense. The dead of this period will be the accusers of the man responsible for the continuation of that fight, Adolf Hitler, just as much as the destroyed cities, destroyed in that last phase, who had lost tremendous cultural values and tremendous numbers of dwellings. . . . The German people remained faithful to Adolf Hitler until the end. He has betrayed them knowingly. He has tried to throw them into the abyss.

. . . Hitler ordered everyone else to fight to the last and then retreated into death by his own hand. But he left life as he lived it, a deceiver; he left the official report that he had died in battle. This was the man whom these defendants exalted to a Fuhrer. It was they who conspired to get him absolute authority over all of Germany. And in the end he and the system they created for him brought the ruin of them all. As stated by Speer on cross-examination:

> the tremendous danger, however, contained in this totalitarian system only became abundantly clear at the moment when we were approaching the end. It was then that one

could see what the meaning of the principle was, namely, that every order should be carried out without any criticism. Everything . . . you have seen in the way of orders which were carried out without any consideration, did after all turn out to be mistakes. . . . This system—let me put it like this: to the end of the system it had become clear what tremendous dangers are contained in any such system, as such quite apart from Hitler's principle. The combination of Hitler and this system, then, brought about this tremendous catastrophe to this world.

But let me for a moment turn devil's advocate. I admit that Hitler was the chief villain. But for the defendants to put all blame on him is neither manly nor true. We know that even the head of the state has the same limits to his senses and to the hours of his days as do lesser men. He must rely on others to be his eyes and ears as to most that goes on in a great empire. Other legs must run his errands; other hands must execute his plans. On whom did Hitler rely for such things more than upon these men in the dock? Who led him to believe he had an invincible air armada if not [Hermann] Goring? Who kept disagreeable facts from him? Did not Goring forbid Field Marshal [Erhard] Milch to warn Hitler that in his opinion Germany was not equal to the war upon Russia? Did not Goring, according to Speer, relieve General [Adolf] Galland of his air force command for speaking of the weaknesses and bungling of the air forces? Who led Hitler, utterly untraveled himself, to believe in the indecision and timidity of democratic peoples if not [Joachim von] Ribbentrop, [Constantin] Von Neurath, and [Franz] Von Papen? Who fed his illusion of German invincibility if not [Wilhelm] Keitel, [Alfred] Jodl, [Erich] Raeder, and [Karl] Donitz? Who kept his hatred of the Jews inflamed more than [Julius] Streicher and [Alfred] Rosenberg? Who would Hitler say deceived him about conditions in concentration camps if not [Ernst] Kaltenbrunner, even as he would deceive us? These men had access to Hitler and often could control the information that reached him and on which he must base his policy and his orders. They were the Praetorian Guard, and while they were under Caesar's orders, Caesar was always in their hands.

Lies and Euphemisms

If these dead men could take the witness stand and answer what has been said against them, we might have a less distorted picture of the parts played by these defendants. Imagine the stir that would occur in the dock if it should behold Adolf Hitler advancing to the witness box, or Himmler with an armful of dossiers, or [Joseph] Goebbels, or [Martin] Bormann with the reports of his Party spies, or the murdered [Ernst] Rohm or [Wilhelm] Canaris. The ghoulish defense that the world is entitled to retribution only from the cadavers is an argument worthy of the crimes at which it is directed. We have presented to this Tribunal an affirmative case based on incriminating documents which are sufficient, if unexplained, to require a finding of guilt on Count One against each defendant. In the final analysis, the only question is whether the defendant's own testimony is to be credited as against the documents and other evidence of their guilt. What, then, is their testimony worth? The fact is that the Nazi habit of economizing in the use of truth pulls the foundations out from under their own defenses.

Lying has always been a highly approved Nazi technique. Hitler, in *Mein Kampf,* advocated mendacity as a policy. Von Ribbentrop admits the use of the "diplomatic lie." Keitel advised that the facts of rearmament be kept secret so that they could be denied at Geneva. Raeder deceived about rebuilding the German Navy in violation of Versailles. Goring urged Ribbentrop to tell a "legal lie" to the British Foreign Office about the Anschluss [the German annexation of Austria], and in so doing only marshaled him the way he was going. Goring gave his word of honor to the Czechs and proceeded to break it. Even Speer proposed to deceive the French into revealing the specially trained among their prisoners.

Nor is the direct lie the only means of falsehood. They all speak with a Nazi double talk with which to deceive the unwary. In the Nazi dictionary of sardonic euphemisms "final solution" of the Jewish problem was a phrase which meant extermination; "special treatment" of prisoners of war meant killing; "protective custody" meant concentration camp; "duty labor" meant slave labor; and an order to "take a firm attitude" or "take positive measures" meant to act with unrestrained savagery. Before we accept their word at what seems to be its face, we must always look for hidden meanings. Goring assured us, on his oath, that the Reich Defense Council never met "as such." When we produced the stenographic minutes of a meeting at which he presided and did most of the talking, he reminded us of the "as such" and explained this was not a meeting of the Council "as such" because other persons were present. Goring denies "threatening" Czechoslovakia; he only told President [Emil] Hacha that he would "hate to bomb the beautiful city of Prague." Besides outright false statements and double talk, there are also other circumventions of truth in the nature of fantastic explanations and absurd professions. Streicher has solemnly maintained that his only thought with respect to the Jews was to resettle them on the island of Madagascar. His reason for destroying synagogues he blandly said, was only because they were architecturally offensive. Rosenberg was stated by his counsel to have always had in mind a "chivalrous solution" to the Jewish problem. When it was necessary to remove [Austrian chancellor Kurt von] Schuschnigg after the Anschluss, Ribbentrop would have had us believe that the Austrian Chancellor was resting at a "villa." It was left to cross-examination to reveal that the "villa" was Buchenwald Concentration Camp. The record is full of other examples of dissimulations and evasions. Even Schacht showed that he, too, had adopted the Nazi attitude that truth is any story which succeeds. Confronted on cross-examination with a long record of broken vows and false words, he declared in justification and I quote from the record:

> I think you can score many more successes when you want to lead someone if you don't tell them the truth than if you tell them the truth.

This was the philosophy of the National Socialists. When for years they have deceived the world, and masked falsehood with plausibilities, can anyone be surprised that they continue their habits of a lifetime in this dock? Credibility is one of the main issues of this Trial. Only those who have failed to learn the bitter lessons of the last decade can doubt that men who have always played on the unsuspecting credulity of generous opponents would not hesitate to do the same, now.

It is against such a background that these defendants now ask this Tribunal to say that they are not guilty of planning, executing, or conspiring to commit this long list of crimes and wrongs. They stand before the record of this Trial as bloodstained Gloucester stood by the body of his slain king. He begged of the widow, as they beg of you: "Say I slew them not." And the Queen replied, "Then say they were not slain. But dead they are. . . ." If you were to say of these men that they are not guilty, it would be as true to say that there has been no war, there are no slain, there has been no crime.

The Marshall Plan

George C. Marshall

World War II left the countries of Europe devastated, with hundreds of cities in ruins, industries destroyed, transportation and infrastructure extensively damaged, and desperate populations struggling against starvation and hopelessness. The victorious leaders of the West knew that the legacy of World War I must not be repeated—that economic vengeance should not be exacted by the Allies from the Axis powers, and thus potentially bring about another generation of tyranny and fanaticism to plague Europe.

As proposed by the United States, the solution to postwar reconstruction was known as the Marshall Plan, named for Secretary of State George C. Marshall, who had led the United States to victory as army chief of staff. In the following commencement speech given at Harvard University on June 5, 1947, Marshall outlined the case for economic aid and cooperation with the European nations, both Allied and Axis. Political stability and a healthy, interdependent economy were the primary goals.

The Marshall Plan was given its legislative framework in the next year by the Economic Cooperation Act of 1948, which extended economic assistance to war-torn Europe. The Marshall Plan helped to rebuild the nations of Western Europe, but also strengthened the U.S. military and political alliances, with these nations. It formed a vital support for the postwar anti-Soviet alliance known as the North Atlantic Treaty Organization (NATO), and earned Marshall himself a Nobel Peace Prize in 1953.

Excerpted from George C. Marshall's commencement address given at Harvard University, June 5, 1947.

I need not tell you, gentlemen, that the world situation is very serious. That must be apparent to all intelligent people. I think one difficulty is that the problem is one of such enormous complexity that the very mass of facts presented to the public by press and radio make it exceedingly difficult for the man in the street to reach a clear appraisement of the situation. Furthermore, the people of this country are distant from the troubled areas of the earth and it is hard for them to comprehend the plight and consequent reactions of the long-suffering peoples, and the effect of those reactions on their governments in connection with our efforts to promote peace in the world.

In considering the requirements for the rehabilitation of Europe, the physical loss of life, the visible destruction of cities, factories, mines and railroads was correctly estimated but it has become obvious during recent months that this visible destruction was probably less serious than the dislocation of the entire fabric of European economy. For the past 10 years conditions have been highly abnormal. The feverish preparation for war and the more feverish maintenance of the war effort engulfed all aspects of national economies. Machinery has fallen into disrepair or is entirely obsolete. Under the arbitrary and destructive Nazi rule, virtually every possible enterprise was geared into the German war machine. Long-standing commercial ties, private institutions, banks, insurance companies, and shipping companies disappeared, through loss of capital, absorption through nationalization, or by simple destruction. In many countries, confidence in the local currency has been severely shaken. The breakdown of the business structure of Europe during the war was complete. Recovery has been seriously retarded by the fact that two years after the close of hostilities a peace settlement with Germany and Austria has not been agreed upon. But even given a more prompt solution of these difficult problems the rehabilitation of the economic structure of Europe quite evidently will require a much longer time and greater effort than had been foreseen.

There is a phase of this matter which is both interesting and serious. The farmer has always produced the foodstuffs to exchange with the city dweller for the other necessities of life. This division of labor is the basis of modern civilization. At the present time it is threatened with breakdown. The town and city industries are not producing adequate goods to exchange with the food producing farmer. Raw materials and fuel are in short supply. Machinery is lacking or worn out. The farmer or the peasant cannot find the goods for sale which he desires to purchase. So the sale of his farm produce for money which he cannot use seems to him an unprofitable transaction. He, therefore, has withdrawn many fields from crop cultivation and is using them for grazing. He feeds more grain to stock and finds for himself and his family an ample supply of food, however short he may be on clothing and the other ordinary gadgets of civilization. Meanwhile people in the cities are short of food and fuel. So the governments are forced to use their foreign money and credits to procure these necessities abroad. This process exhausts funds which are urgently needed for reconstruction. Thus a very serious situation is rapidly developing which bodes no good for the world. The modern system of the division of labor upon which the exchange of products is based is in danger of breaking down.

The truth of the matter is that Europe's requirements for the next three or four years of foreign food and other essential products—principally from America—are so much greater than her present ability to pay that she must have substantial additional help or face economic, social, and political deterioration of a very grave character.

The remedy lies in breaking the vicious circle and restoring the confidence of the European people in the economic future of their own countries and of Europe as a whole. The manufacturer and the farmer throughout wide areas must be able and willing to exchange their products for currencies the continuing value of which is not open to question.

Aside from the demoralizing effect on the world at large and the possibilities of disturbances arising as a result of the desperation of the people concerned, the consequences to the economy of the United States should be apparent to all. It is logical that the United States should do whatever it is able to do to assist in the return of normal economic health in the world, without which there can be no political stability and no assured peace. Our policy is directed not against any country or doctrine but against hunger, poverty, desperation and chaos. Its purpose should be the revival of a working economy in the world so as to permit the emergence of political and social conditions in which free institutions can exist. Such assistance, I am convinced, must not be on a piecemeal basis as various crises develop. Any assistance that this Government may render in the future should provide a cure rather than a mere palliative. Any government that is willing to assist in the task of recovery will find full co-operation I am sure, on the part of the United States Government. Any government which maneuvers to block the recovery of other countries cannot expect help from us. Furthermore, governments, political parties, or groups which seek to perpetuate human misery in order to profit therefrom politically or otherwise will encounter the opposition of the United States.

It is already evident that, before the United States Government can proceed much further in its efforts to alleviate the situation and help start the European world on its way to recovery, there must be some agreement among the countries of Europe as to the requirements of the situation and the part those countries themselves will take in order to give proper effect to whatever action might be undertaken by this Government. It would be neither fitting nor efficacious for this Government to undertake to draw up unilaterally a program designed to place Europe on its feet economically. This is the business of the Europeans. The initiative, I think, must come from Europe. The role of this country should consist of friendly aid in the drafting of a European program and of later support of such a program so far as it may be practical for us to do so. The program should be a joint one, agreed to by a number, if not all European nations.

An essential part of any successful action on the part of the United States is an understanding on the part of the people of America of the character of the problem and the remedies to be applied. Political passion and prejudice should have no part. With foresight, and a willingness on the part of our people to face up to the vast responsibility which history has clearly placed upon our country, the difficulties I have outlined can and will be overcome.

Appendix of Biographies

A.K. Cajander

Cajander served three different terms as prime minister of Finland: from June 6 until November 14, 1922 (in a caretaker government); from January 18 until May 31, 1924; and finally from March 12, 1937, until December 1, 1939. He was considered somewhat of a pacifist during the 1930s, a time when he cut Finnish defense spending while the rest of Europe, and Germany in particular, were rearming. Cajander is best remembered for his speech of November 23, 1939, in which he defied the threats and demands for territorial and port concessions made by the Soviet Union in the fall of 1939. He resigned one week later, just after the Soviet Union attacked Finland, beginning the "Winter War" that would end with a truce favorable to the Soviet Union in March 1940.

Neville Chamberlain

Chamberlain was born in Birmingham, England, in 1869. He attended Rugby School and afterward moved to the Bahamas, where he managed a family estate. He returned to England in 1897 and in 1915 was elected as the lord-mayor of Birmingham, an industrial city in the English Midlands. Appointed head of the British conscription service in 1917, he was elected as a Conservative member of Parliament in 1918. He was appointed as chancellor of the exchequer and postmaster general from 1923 until 1924 and as minister of health from 1923 until 1929. He rose to chancellor of the exchequer in 1931, in the government of Ramsay MacDonald.

On the resignation of Stanley Baldwin in 1937, Chamberlain became prime minister. He favored a policy of granting concessions to Italy and Germany in hopes of avoiding war. This policy was opposed by prominent British politicians, including most notably Winston Churchill. In 1936, Chamberlain had agreed to the Italian conquest of Ethiopia. At the Munich Conference in September 1938, Chamberlain also agreed to the concession of the Sudetenland, a German-speaking portion of Czechoslovakia, to Nazi Germany. This appeasement did not stop German designs on Czechoslovakia, as Hitler ordered the full occupation of the country in March 1939. The policy of appeasement had failed; on the invasion of Poland in September, Chamberlain and the British government declared war on Germany. Early the next year, after the

British suffered defeat in Norway and members of the opposition parties refused to serve in his government, Chamberlain resigned his post. Prime Minister Winston Churchill, who succeeded Chamberlain, named him lord president, a ceremonial post which he resigned from due to poor health in October 1940. Chamberlain died on November 9, 1940.

Chiang Kai-shek

Chiang was a Chinese Nationalist leader who fought against the Chinese Communists as well as the Japanese through the 1930s and during the course of World War II. After receiving military training in the Japanese army, Chiang played an active role in the revolution against the Manchus, China's last imperial dynasty. Under the government of Sun Yat-Sen, established in 1917, Chiang served as military advisor. In 1924 he was named as the head of a military school at Whampoa. In 1926, he led an expedition of Chinese Nationalists against the major cities of Nanking and Shanghai. He broke with the Communists, with whom the Nationalists had been cooperating, in 1927. As head of the Kuomintang, or Chinese Nationalist army, he rose to head of the Nationalist government in 1928. The civil war between the Nationalists and Communists dragged on through the early 1930s as imperial Japan attacked and conquered large swaths of northern China. In 1937, a second war with Japan broke out. The Japanese eventually captured Nanking, the Nationalist capital, and forced Chiang to flee.

Chiang and the Kuomintang leaders were cultivated by the Allied nations in their fight against Japanese domination of eastern Asia. Under pressure from British forces in southern Asia and the United States in the Pacific, Japan eventually withdrew from China and finally surrendered in August 1945. After the war ended, the Kuomintang and the Communists resumed their war. Chiang was elected as the president of China in 1948 but soon afterward resigned. In 1949 a Communist offensive drove the Nationalists out of mainland China; they eventually took refuge on Taiwan. The Nationalist government survived under Chiang's leadership until his death in 1975.

Winston Churchill

Churchill was born into the English nobility, the son of Lord Randolph Churchill and Jennie Jerome, an American. Churchill attended Harrow and Sandhurst, a military academy, and was commissioned an officer in the Fourth Hussars in 1894. He served as a military observer in Cuba, and took part in campaigns in India and the Sudan, where he participated in the Battle of Omdurman in 1898. After resigning his commission, he became a war correspondent, rising to public notice with his reports from the Boer War. He became a Conservative member of Parliament in 1900 but later changed allegiance to the Liberal party. During the Asquith government, he served as president of the Board of Trade and, from 1910 until 1911, home secretary. He became lord of the admiralty in 1911 and oversaw the British naval buildup in preparation for war with Germany.

Churchill resigned his post after the ill-fated Dardanelles campaign in 1915, which he had helped to plan. After World War I he served as colonial secretary and, from 1924 until 1929, as chancellor of the exchequer. During the 1930s, Churchill was out of office, although he remained in the public eye with several books of history and his untiring warning of the menace posed by Hitler and Nazi Germany. Prime Minister Neville Chamberlain appointed him lord of the admiralty in September 1939 after the outbreak of World War II. Churchill succeeded Chamberlain in May 1940 and served as prime minister throughout the war. His speeches, which expressed his determination to fight Germany despite devastating air attacks and the threat of invasion, inspired the British to fight on and were widely credited with helping defeat Hitler. Churchill tirelessly traveled the front lines as well as the Allied capitals, planning strategy for the war as well as the ensuing peace. In July 1945, the Labour party won a majority in Parliament and Churchill became the opposition leader.

Churchill predicted the postwar conflict between western Europe and the Soviet Union with a famous speech delivered at Fulton, Missouri, in 1946. He coined the phrase "Iron Curtain," a political, economic, and cultural barrier that divided the West and Communist Europe. He served again as prime minister from 1951 to 1955. He was renowned throughout the world for his speeches as well as his books and won the Nobel Prize in literature in 1953.

Édouard Daladier

Daladier was French premier during the 1930s and at the start of World War II. A radical Socialist, Daladier was first elected to the national legislature in 1919 and held several posts in the French Cabinet of Ministers through the 1920s. He served as prime minister in 1933, 1934, and again in 1938, when the German military buildup and the Anschluss made it apparent that war with Germany was approaching. Nevertheless, he signed the Munich Agreement in September 1938, which allowed Germany to occupy the

Sudetenland region of Czechoslovakia. At the start of the war, he held the premiership as well as the post of minister of war and of foreign affairs. On the invasion and defeat of France in 1940, he was ousted and thereafter arrested by the collaborationist government at Vichy, which ruled the southern half of France. He was arrested and imprisoned by the Germans in 1942. After the war, he testified against Marshal Petain, the Vichy president, and regained his seat in the National Assembly, where he remained until 1958.

Charles de Gaulle

The son of a French officer, de Gaulle graduated from St. Cyr, the leading French military academy, in 1911. He fought in World War I until his capture at Verdun in 1916. After the war, he taught at St. Cyr and held a series of high-ranking army posts. In 1934, he promoted the concept of mechanized warfare in a book entitled *The Army of the Future.*

De Gaulle held command of a French armored division during the German invasion of France in the spring of 1940. He fled to England after the surrender of France and refused to recognize the Vichy government, for which he was sentenced to death in absentia. While in England, he organized the free French resistance forces and became president of the French National Committee in September 1941. The Allies accepted him as the leader of the French resistance forces and, in June 1944, he took command of the provisional government, known as the French Committee of National Liberation. He marched at the front of the allied armies after the withdrawal of the Germans from Paris in the summer of 1944.

After the war, de Gaulle organized a strongly nationalistic political party known as the Rassemblement du Peuple Francais, or Rally of the French Nation. In 1958, during a coup of French officers in the colony of Algeria, de Gaulle formed a new government, oversaw the writing of a new constitution, and established the Fifth Republic. He was elected as the Fifth Republic's first president in 1958. After Algerian independence in 1962, de Gaulle brought France out of NATO, the postwar Atlantic alliance led by the United States, and established France as an independent military power in Europe. He won a second term as president in 1965 but resigned in April 1969.

Francisco Franco

In 1924 Franco, the son of a Spanish naval officer, was trained at the Toledo Academy. He served in the Spanish colony of Morocco from 1912 until 1927, reaching the rank of general and the post of commander of the Moroccan Legion in 1924. Franco supported the conservative faction in Spain's increasingly bitter political disputes during the early 1930s, which were touched off by the abdication of King Alfonso XIII in 1931. In 1935 he was named chief of staff in the Spanish army; in the following year a new leftist government sent him to a post in the distant Canary Islands.

In July 1936, conservative officers staged a revolt against the government of Spain. Franco left for Morocco, took command of a large, supportive army, and joined the rebellion in Spain. Within three months he was named commander in chief of the Nationalist faction. He organized the various Nationalist parties into the Falange, the fascist party that swept away their Loyalist opponents by 1939, when Franco was installed as Spain's permanent dictator. During World War II, Spain was officially neutral but gave military and political support to the Axis. An international pariah immediately after the war, Franco's strong anti-Communism earned him a military and economic alliance with the United States in 1953. In 1969, he named Prince Juan Carlos, the grandson of Alfonso XIII, as the monarch to succeed him, preparing a peaceful transformation from dictatorship to constitutional monarchy which took place in 1975.

Mohandas Gandhi

Gandhi was the son of an Indian government official. In 1888, he moved to England, where he studied law, then returned to India in 1891. He moved to South Africa in 1893 and worked on behalf of ethnic Indians, many of whom suffered discrimination at the hands of the British colonial authorities. He gradually gave up the trappings of middle-class life and adopted the customs and dress of a wandering ascetic. He also began organizing campaigns of nonviolent civil disobedience to protest what he saw as unjust laws and practices. In 1915 he returned to India, still a British colony, where he soon became a hero among Indians fighting for independence.

Gandhi rose to a place of honor in the National Congress, the political party fighting for a sovereign and independent Indian nation. After a well-publicized protest against British salt taxes in 1930, he was imprisoned for seven months. Although he split with the National Congress in the 1930s, he remained at the forefront of the independence movement. In 1942, he offered to support the British in their war against Germany in exchange for independence, but was refused. The British held him under house arrest at the palace of Aga Khan in Poona until 1944. After the war, the British withdrew from India but also partitioned the country into separate, predominantly Hindu (India) and Muslim (Pakistan) countries. Gandhi strongly opposed the partition and campaigned for reunification of the two populations, but was rebuffed by Hindu nationalists, one of whom assassinated him on January 30, 1948.

Naruhiko Higashikuni

Born in a Kyoto prefecture, Prince Higashikuni led, with the deposed premier Prince Konoye, a pacifist faction of the Japanese government that opposed the militaristic and expansionist policies of Hideki Tojo. As the American forces progressed across the Pacific Ocean in 1944, the Japanese defeats brought scandal on Tojo's military and an opportunity for Higashikuni and his political allies. After the fall of the Marianas Islands in July 1944, Higashikuni's faction pressed Emperor Hirohito to force Tojo out of power. This was achieved on July 18, when Tojo's resignation was accepted by the emperor. Higashikuni was elevated to the post of prime minister of Japan on August 17, 1945, after the atomic bombing of Hiroshima and Nagasaki. He presided over the Japanese surrender in the following weeks and resigned his post on October 9, 1945.

Heinrich Himmler

Born in Munich, in southern Germany, Himmler enthusiastically supported Adolf Hitler and Germany's National Socialist (Nazi) party, which was formed in the early 1920s. In 1929, Hitler appointed him as the head of the Schutzstaffel (SS, or "blackshirts"), an organization that originally served as Hitler's bodyguard service, but which gradually expanded into an elite Nazi police force. In 1930, Himmler was elected as a Nazi deputy to the German Reichstag (legislature). In 1933, Adolf Hitler became chancellor of Germany. Mistrusting the SA militia (or "brownshirts"), the principle rival to the SS, Hitler arranged for a purge and murder of the SA leaders in 1934 and made Himmler's SS the most powerful single organization in Nazi Germany. In 1936 Himmler was appointed as the chief of all police organizations in Germany.

After World War II broke out in 1939, the SS was charged with occupying and policing conquered territories throughout Europe. Under Himmler's direction, the SS set up concentration camps for political prisoners and extermination camps for the purpose of cleansing the expanding German realm of undesirable ethnic minorities, including Jews and Gypsies. Himmler's power increased as the war continued, as Germany began to suffer setbacks on its western and eastern fronts, and as Hitler became increasingly suspicious of his allies and subordinates. In the final days of the war Himmler was captured; he committed suicide while in custody.

Hirohito

The son of Japan's Emperor Yoshihito, Hirohito was named crown prince in 1912 and attained the imperial throne in 1926. Hirohito favored a moderate policy in which all political factions would be allowed a voice in the Japanese government. During his reign, however, an increasingly militant and belligerent faction rose to power in the Japanese cabinet, staging a coup in 1936 that was only put down through the emperor's influence.

Japan pursued a policy of invasion and expansion in eastern Asia. In August 1945, after the atomic bombing of Hiroshima and Nagasaki, Hirohito prevailed on his cabinet to accept the Allied terms of surrender. After the formal surrender, Hirohito was allowed his freedom and his imperial title, but was stripped of all effective authority and made a figurehead. During the 1970s, Hirohito became the first Japanese emperor to travel outside his country. On his death in 1989, he was succeeded by his son, Prince Akihito.

Adolf Hitler

The son of a customs official, Adolf Hitler moved to Vienna, the capital of Austria, in 1907. He joined the German army at the beginning of World War I. After suffering gas poisoning in northern France, he was awarded the Iron Cross. After the war, he joined the German Workers' party, which became the National Socialist German Workers' party in 1920. Hitler rose to become the party leader and instilled his extreme brand of nationalism in a small group of followers. A Nazi coup attempt in Munich in 1923 failed, however, and for his part in the coup Hitler was jailed for nine months.

After his release, Hitler and his party gained support among those unhappy with Germany's defeat and humiliation in World War I and with the country's severe economic crisis. Hitler finally gained control in the German government in 1933, when President Paul von Hindenburg named Hitler as the chancellor, or prime minister, of Germany. Hitler established a Nazi dictatorship, purged the country of his political enemies, and rebuilt the German army and navy in violation of the Treaty of Versailles, the agreement Germany had signed after World War I.

Proclaiming the establishment of a Third Reich (or empire) under his personal leadership, Hitler ordered the invasion and occupation of Czechoslovakia, Austria, and Poland. The conquest of

Poland touched off World War II in September 1939. Germany conquered much of western Europe in 1940 and then opened a second front in the east by attacking the Soviet Union in 1941. The Allies, who opposed the Axis alliance dominated by Germany, were joined by the United States in December 1941, and defeated Germany by May 1945. On April 30, a week before the formal surrender, Hitler committed suicide in an underground bunker in Berlin, the German capital.

Robert H. Jackson

Born in Spring Creek, Pennsylvania, Jackson passed the New York state bar in 1913, after which he practiced law in Jamestown, New York. During the 1930s, he worked for the Internal Revenue Service as a general counsel and in the U.S. Department of Justice's antitrust division. As U.S. attorney general, a post to which he was appointed in 1940, he made the legal case for the Lend-Lease program, in which U.S. warships were lent in exchange for U.S. military bases leased in Great Britain and its colonies. In 1941 he was appointed to the U.S. Supreme Court. He was asked to serve as the chief prosecutor at the International War Crimes Tribunals in Nuremberg, Germany, from 1945 to 1946, and during this time wrote a book on the trials, *The Case Against the Nazi War Criminals*. Among scholars of the American justice system, he is best known for his book *The Supreme Court in the American System of Government*, which was published shortly after his death in 1954.

George C. Marshall

Born in Pennsylvania and a graduate of the Virginia Military Institute, Marshall served as an army officer in the First Infantry Division during World War I. After the war, he was appointed as an aide to General John "Black Jack" Pershing. Marshall served in China during the 1920s and, under the Depression-era Roosevelt administration, organized the Civilian Conservation Corps. He was appointed army chief of staff in 1939 and as general of the army in 1944. Marshall directed the overall U.S. military strategy in World War II, including a plan for the reconquest of Europe via an invasion of northern France. After the war, he retired as chief of staff and was appointed as a special ambassador to China, where he unsuccessfully tried to form a coalition government to end the civil war between China's Nationalist and Communist factions.

Marshall was named secretary of state by President Truman in January 1947. In that year he led the effort of the reconstruction of Europe through the European Recovery Program, also known as the Marshall Plan. He resigned his post in January 1949 but was recalled as secretary of defense in September 1951, during the Korean War. In 1953, he won the Nobel Peace Prize for the Marshall Plan's economic rebuilding of Europe.

Benito Mussolini

Born in the Forli region of Italy, Mussolini joined the Socialist party and emigrated to Switzerland from 1902 until 1904. He spoke out forcefully against militarism and promoted a Socialist revolution to sweep away what he saw as Italy's antiquated and corrupt government institutions. In 1913, he became editor of *Avanti,* the Socialist party newspaper.

Mussolini decided to support Italy's participation in World War I on the side of the Allies. This stand brought a permanent break with the Socialist party. In 1914 he founded his own newspaper, the *Popolo d'Italia*, and in 1915 he joined the army. He changed his philosophy to one of extreme nationalism and militarism, and formed an Italian fascist party. Popularly known as the "Blackshirts," Mussolini's followers marched on Rome in October 1922 to challenge and overthrow the country's weak liberal government. After a long period of political anarchy, the king of Italy invited Mussolini to form a new government. Mussolini attained the post of prime minister and proceeded to establish a fascist dictatorship, naming himself Il Duce (the leader). In 1929, he offered a generous Concordat to the Vatican, establishing a close alliance with the Roman Catholic hierarchy.

In 1935, Mussolini ordered the invasion of Ethiopia, an action that stemmed criticism and an economic crisis within Italy. He formed the Rome-Berlin Axis with Hitler's Germany, joined the war as an ally of Germany, and ordered attacks on Albania, Greece, and North Africa. All three campaigns brought humiliating defeats, however, and Mussolini fell from power in July 1943. He was captured and executed by pro-Allied Italian partisans on April 28, 1945.

George S. Patton

Born in San Gabriel, California, Patton graduated from West Point in 1909. In 1916, he served as an aide to General John Pershing during a military foray into Mexico during the Mexican Revolution. Patton also commanded a U.S. tank brigade in World War I. In 1941 he was commander of the army's Second Armored Division. In 1942 he led the First Armored Corps in the U.S. invasion of North Africa. After this mission he was given command of the

Seventh Army during the invasion of Sicily. In frequent conflict with his superior officers, particularly Supreme Allied Commander Dwight Eisenhower, Patton was later relieved from command of the Seventh Army.

Patton was later given command of the Third Army and was promoted to the rank of major general in August 1944. His forces fought across northern France, played a key role in the Battle of the Bulge, which took place in late 1944, and ended the war in southern Germany. Patton was named military governor of the U.S. sector in southern Germany but was relieved of this post in October 1945. He died two months later from injuries suffered in a car accident.

Franklin D. Roosevelt

Born into a wealthy New York family, Roosevelt attended Harvard University and Columbia University School of Law. He was elected the Democratic candidate to the New York legislature in 1910 and was a staunch supporter of Woodrow Wilson, who won election as president in 1912. In the Wilson administration Roosevelt served as assistant secretary of the navy. He ran for vice president in 1920, but in that year the Republican ticket, with Warren Harding at its head, defeated the Democrats.

In 1921 Roosevelt contracted polio, which confined him to a wheelchair for the rest of his life. In 1928 and 1930 he was elected governor of New York, promoting legislation that regulated business and utilities and provided expanded social benefits. In 1932, the worst year of the Great Depression, he was elected president. The Roosevelt administration promoted the "New Deal"—laws to shore up the banking system, regulate stock markets, and combat widespread joblessness with government employment and relief programs.

Roosevelt was reelected in 1936 and 1940. After the outbreak of World War II, his administrated supported a rapid rearmament of the U.S. military. He asked for, and immediately received, a declaration of war against the Axis on December 8, 1941, the day after the Japanese attack on Pearl Harbor. In 1944, as the fortunes of war turned against the Axis, he met with other Allied leaders in a series of important conferences to shape the postwar world. On April 12, 1945, as Allied forces were driving across a defeated Germany, he died from a stroke.

Haile Selassie

Born Tafari Makonnen, Selassie was a grand-nephew of Ethiopia's Emperor Menilek II. The emperor named him governor of Sidamo province in 1912. In the next year, Menilek died and was succeeded by his grandson, Lij Yasu, a Muslim rival of the Christian Lij Tafari. Tafari successfully ousted Lij Yasu and established himself as regent in 1916 for Zauditu, the daughter of Menilek. Tafari took control of the Ethiopian army in 1926 and in 1928 was crowned king. In 1930, after the death of Zauditu, he was crowned sole emperor, an event he commemorated by renaming himself Haile Selassie ("Power of the Trinity").

Upon Italy's invasion and conquest of Ethiopia, the emperor fled his homeland to appeal for aid from the League of Nations, which did nothing. In 1941, with Italy suffering military setbacks in Europe and North Africa, he returned to Ethiopia, which was reconquered by Ethiopian partisans working in concert with a British army. After the war, he undertook the modernization of the country, allowed the formation of a representative assembly, and oversaw Ethiopia's first elections in 1957. But opposition to his authoritarian reign grew among officers in the Ethiopian army. In 1974, he was overthrown in a military coup. He died in captivity the next year.

Joseph Stalin

The son of a Georgian shoemaker, Stalin studied for the priesthood but was expelled from his seminary. He joined the local Social Democratic party and Lenin's Bolshevik faction in 1903, after a split in the national party. He carried out various clandestine activities, including sabotage and bank robberies, on behalf of the party, and was appointed to the party's central committee before his arrest and exile to Siberia in 1913. He was granted a pardon in 1917 and left for St. Petersburg, the Russian imperial capital, where he became an editor for *Pravda*, the Bolshevik newspaper. The Bolsheviks seized power in October 1917, and renamed themselves the Communist party.

In 1922 Stalin rose to the rank of general secretary of the party. When Lenin died, Stalin found himself in a rivalry with Trotsky, another leading Bolshevik, in the contest for succession as head of the party. Stalin's maneuvers behind the scenes eventually forced Trotsky into exile and many of Stalin's other enemies into prison or before a firing squad. Stalin directed the ruthless collectivization of agriculture and crash industrialization of the Soviet Union during the 1930s. During this time, he also ordered the arrest, trial, and execution of millions of Soviet officials, military officers, and ordinary citizens.

Stalin signed a treaty with Adolf Hitler on the eve of World War

II that allowed the Soviet Union control over half of Poland as well as the Baltic States. But the Nazi leader ordered an invasion of the Soviet Union in June 1941. The war devastated the western reaches of the Soviet Union and killed around 20 million Soviet soldiers and citizens. Seeking to extend the Soviet sphere of influence after the war, Stalin ordered the creation of subservient Communist governments in central Europe. He also broke with an independent Communist government in Yugoslavia and with Communist China.

Hideki Tojo

The son of a Japanese general, Tojo trained for a military career. He favored Japanese expansion in Asia, and during the 1930s gradually took the upper hand in a chaotic and divided Japanese government. He rose to chief of staff in Manchuria, the Japanese-held region of northern China, in 1935. He attained the cabinet in 1940 as the minister of war. In October 1941, he maneuvered Prince Konoye, the Japanese prime minister, out of his post and took over leadership of the Japanese government. Tojo gave the final order to carry out the attack on Pearl Harbor on January 7, 1941, an event that brought the United States into the war against Germany and Japan.

Under Tojo's direction, Japan attacked southeast Asia, the Philippines, and U.S. bases in the western Pacific. The defeats that began with the Battle of Midway in 1942, however, weakened his popularity, and in July 1944, he resigned after the United States captured the strategically important island of Saipan. After the Japanese surrender, he was arrested and tried by the United States and executed in 1948.

Harry S. Truman

Born in Lamar, Missouri, Truman grew up on a farm and attended school in the town of Independence. Although his poor vision kept him out of West Point, he joined the U.S. Army in 1917 and served in northern France as an artillery officer during World War I. In 1922 he was elected as a judge in Jackson County, Missouri, with the help of Thomas Pendergast, the Democratic party boss of Kansas City. With Pendergast's support, Truman was elected to the U.S. Senate in 1934. An enthusiastic supporter of President Franklin D. Roosevelt's New Deal policies, Truman joined the Senate Interstate Commerce Committee. From 1941 until 1944, he chaired the "Truman committee" to investigate waste and fraud in defense spending. The reputation for honesty he gained through these assignments persuaded Roosevelt to name Truman as his running mate in 1944. Upon Roosevelt's death on April 12, 1945, Vice

President Truman became president. In August, he authorized the dropping of two atomic bombs on Japan, an act that persuaded Japan's leaders to surrender.

Truman directed U.S. foreign policy in the postwar years with an eye to rebuilding Japan and Europe. Truman countered the influence of the Soviet Union during this time with the Marshall Plan, a program of financial aid, loans and credits intended to help European countries allied to the United States rebuild after the war. He was reelected in 1948; in 1950 he ordered U.S. troops to Korea to fight an invasion by Communist-led North Korea of the U.S.-allied South Korea. During this conflict, he broke with General Douglas MacArthur over the proper direction of the war. MacArthur favored a direct attack on China, North Korea's ally, while Truman opposed this course. The dispute ended with Truman dismissing MacArthur from his post.

Chronology

1931
September 18: Japan invades Manchuria, the northern region of China.

1936
March 7: In violation of the Treaty of Versailles, the German government orders a military occupation of the west bank of the Rhine River.

May: Italy conquers Ethiopia.

July: Republican forces battle the Falange party, led by Francisco Franco, as the Spanish Civil War erupts.

1937
July 7: Japan invades China.

1938
March 12: The Anschluss, or annexation of Austria, begins as German armies march into Austria at the invitation of the Austrian prime minister, Seyss-Inquart.

September 30: By the Munich Agreement, Germany is allowed to annex the Sudetenland, a German-speaking region of Czechoslovakia.

1939
March 15: German troops invade the portion of Czechoslovakia not already occupied.

May 22: Germany and Italy sign a treaty of alliance.

August 23: Germany and the Soviet Union sign a peace treaty; in a secret protocol, the two governments agree to divide the territory of Poland between them.

August 25: The British government signs a treaty of mutual assistance with Poland.

September 1: Germany invades Poland.

September 3: Great Britain and France declare war on Germany; Britain announces a naval blockade of Germany.

September 17: The Soviet Union invades Poland.

September 27: Warsaw, the capital of Poland, falls to the German army.

October 31: A German submarine torpedoes the American destroyer *Reuben James,* the first U.S. naval vessel lost in the war.

November 30: The Soviet Union attacks Finland.

1940

March 12: After four months of fighting, in which Finnish armies fight the Red Army to a stalemate, Finland signs a peace agreement with the Soviet Union.

April 9: Germany invades Denmark and begins air and naval assaults on Norway.

May 10: Germany invades France, Belgium, the Netherlands, and Luxembourg.

May 15: The Netherlands surrenders to Germany.

May 26: The evacuation of British and other Allied units from the French port of Dunkerque begins.

May 28: Belgium surrenders to Germany.

June 10: Norway surrenders to Germany; Italy declares war on Great Britain and France.

June 14: The French capital of Paris falls to the German army.

June 18: The Soviet army enters the Baltic States of Estonia, Latvia, and Lithuania.

June 22: Germany and France sign an armistice in the forest of Compiegne, the site of German surrender at the end of World War I.

July 10: German bombers begin daylight attacks on Great Britain, starting the Battle of Britain.

August 25: British forces begin bombing runs over Berlin, the capital of Germany.

September 13: The Italian army invades Egypt, a British colony.

September 22: Japan invades the colony of French Indochina in southeast Asia.

September 27: Germany, Italy, and Japan sign the Tripartite Act, formally establishing the Axis.

October 28: Italy attacks Greece.

November 20: Hungary joins the Axis alliance.

November 23: Romania joins the Axis alliance.

December 9: The British army begins an offensive against Italy in North Africa.

1941

January 22: The Italian-held city of Tobruk, Libya, falls to the British.

April 6: Germany invades Yugoslavia.

April 13: Japan and the Soviet Union sign a treaty of nonaggression.

June 8: British and French armies campaign in Syria.

June 22: Germany attacks the Soviet Union.

August 14: The United States and Britain sign an alliance known as the Atlantic Charter.

August 25: British and Soviet armies occupy Iran to prevent the seizure of vital Persian Gulf oil fields by German armies attacking from southern Russia.

December 7: Japan attacks the U.S. military installations at Pearl Harbor, Hawaii.

December 8: The United States declares war on the Axis powers.

December 9: The Nationalist government of China declares war on the Axis powers.

December 25: The British-held city of Hong Kong surrenders to the Japanese.

1942

January 2: The Japanese capture Manila, the capital of the Philippines.

January 11: The Japanese invade the Dutch East Indies (modern Indonesia).

February 1: The United States counterattacks in the Gilbert and Marshall island groups in the central Pacific.

February 27: The Allies defeat the Japanese at the Battle of the Java Sea in the Dutch East Indies.

April 9: The U.S. military detachment on the island of Bataan, in the Philippines, surrenders to the Japanese.

April 18: A fleet of carrier-based B-25 bombers under Lt. Col. James Doolittle reaches Tokyo and bombs the city for the first time during the war.

June 21: Field Marshal Erwin Rommel and his German Afrika Korps capture Tobruk, Libya.

August 7: The U.S. Marines land on the island of Guadalcanal in the Solomon Islands.

September 16: The German Sixth Army enters Stalingrad, in southern Russia.

November: The Allies lose more than eight hundred thousand tons of shipping to German U-boats, or submarines.

November 7: The Allies carry out Operation Torch, landing in Algeria and Morocco to attack the Afrika Korps from the west.

November 27: While Germany occupies the portion of France it had allowed to remain autonomous, the French navy is scuttled at the port of Toulon.

1943

January 31: The German Sixth Army surrenders at Stalingrad after a bitter winter campaign.

February 8: Guadalcanal falls to the United States after a fierce six-month battle.

July 10: The Allies invade Sicily, which will be lost to the Axis by August 17.

September 3: The Allies land on the Italian mainland at

Messina. On the same day, Italy signs an armistice with the Allies.

October 13: Italy declares war on Germany, its former Axis partner.

November 6: The Soviet army recaptures Kiev, capital of the Ukraine, in the western Soviet Union.

1944

January 27: The Germans lift a nine-hundred-day siege of Leningrad, in the northern Soviet Union.

March 19: Germany invades Hungary to reinforce a puppet government.

March 22: Japan invades India from occupied Burma.

June 4: Rome, Italy, falls to the Allies.

June 6: The Allies land a huge invasion force on the beaches of Normandy, in northern France.

June 13: Germany begins launching V-1 ballistic missiles at England.

July 21: The United States lands on the island of Guam in the Mariana Islands.

August 15: Allied forces land in southern France and begin fighting up the Rhone Valley.

September 10: Finland and the Soviet Union sign an armistice.

October 20: The United States lands in the Philippines.

October 23: The U.S. Navy defeats the Japanese in the Battle of Leyte Gulf, the largest naval battle in history.

December 16: A German counterattack in eastern France begins the Battle of the Bulge.

December 27: The German offensive is stopped and the Allies prepare to invade Germany.

1945

January 9: The Allies invade Luzon, the largest island of the Philippines.

January 11: Warsaw, the capital of Poland, falls to the Soviet army.

January 21: Hungary declares war on Germany.

February 13: The Red Army occupies Budapest, the capital of Hungary.

February 19: U.S. forces begin the fight for the volcanic island of Iwo Jima, south of Tokyo.

April 1: U.S. forces land on Okinawa in the Ryukyu Islands and begin a three-month fight for the island.

April 13: Vienna, the capital of Austria, falls to the Red Army.

April 25: Armies of the United States and the Soviet Union link up at the town of Torgau, Germany.

April 30: Adolf Hitler commits suicide in an underground bunker in Berlin.

May 2: Berlin falls to the Soviet forces.

May 7: Germany surrenders to the Allies at Reims, France.

August 6: The United States drops an atomic bomb on the Japanese city of Hiroshima.

August 9: A second atomic bomb is dropped on Nagasaki.

September 2: Japan formally surrenders to end World War II.

For Further Research

HENRY ADAMS, *1942: The Year That Doomed the Axis.* New York: D. McKay, 1967.

STEPHEN AMBROSE, *Citizen Soldiers: The U.S. Army from Normandy Beaches to the Bulge to the Surrender of Germany, June 7, 1944–May 7, 1945.* New York: Simon and Schuster, 1997.

JAMES BRADLEY AND RON POWERS, *Flags of Our Fathers.* New York: Bantam Books, 2001.

PHILIPPE BURIN, *France Under the Germans: Collaboration and Compromise.* New York: The New Press, 1996.

JOHN CAMPBELL, ED., *The Experience of World War II.* New York: Oxford University Press, 1989.

WINSTON S. CHURCHILL, *The Second World War.* New York: Houghton Mifflin, 1986.

ROBERT COWLEY, ED., *No End Save Victory: Perspectives on World War II.* New York: Penguin USA, 2001.

LEN DEIGHTON, *Blood, Tears, and Folly: An Objective Look at World War II.* New York: HarperCollins, 1993.

DAVID FRASER, *Knights Cross: A Life of Field Marshal Erwin Rommel.* New York: HarperCollins, 1993.

MARTIN GIBERT, *The Holocaust: A History of the Jews of Europe During the Second World War.* New York: Holt, Rinehart & Winston, 1985.

JOHN HERSEY, *Hiroshima.* Thorndike, MD: G.K. Hall, 1994.

JOHN KEEGAN, *The Second World War.* New York: Penguin USA, 1990.

WARREN F. KIMBALL, *Forged in War: Roosevelt, Churchill, and the Second World War.* New York: William Morrow, 1997.

PETER LIDDLE, JOHN BOURNE, AND IAN WHITEHEAD, EDS., *The Great World War, 1914–1945*. London: Harper-Collins, 2000.

DON MCCOMBS AND FRED L. WORTH, *World War II: Strange and Fascinating Facts*. New York: Greenwich House, 1983.

WILLIAMSON MURRAY AND ALLAN R. MILLETT, *A War to Be Won: Fighting the Second World War*. Cambridge, MA: Belknap Press, 2000.

PATRICK K. O'DONNELL, *Into the Rising Sun: In Their Own Words, World War II's Pacific Veterans Reveal the Heart of Combat*. New York: Free Press, 2002.

RICHARD OVERY, *Why the Allies Won*. New York: W.W. Norton, 1996.

RON ROSENBAUM, *Explaining Hitler*. New York: Random House, 1998.

HARRISON SALISBURY, *The 900 Days: The Siege of Leningrad*. New York: Harper and Row, 1969.

WILLIAM L. SHIRER, *The Rise and Fall of the Third Reich: A History of Nazi Germany*. New York: Simon and Schuster, 1990.

HAMPTON SIDES, *Ghost Soldiers: The Forgotten Epic Story of World War II's Most Dramatic Mission*. New York: Doubleday, 2001.

JOHN TOLAND, *Rising Sun: The Decline and Fall of the Japanese Empire, 1936–1945*. New York: Random House, 1970.

RICHARD TREGASKIS, *Guadalcanal Diary*. New York: Random House, 1943.

Index